Audacity

PORTIA TAYLOR

Audacity

Cover by: Morgan 4 Design

Editing: Critique Editing Services

Publisher: Lift Bridge Publishing, LLC

info@liftbridgepublishing.com; www.lbpub.com

Ordering Information: Quantity sales. Special discounts are available on quantity purchases by corporations, associations, and others. For details, contact the publisher at the email above. Orders by U.S. trade bookstores and wholesalers.

Please contact Lift Bridge Publishing:

Tel: (888) 774-9917

King James Version of the bible was used unless otherwise noted and referenced.

Printed in the United States of America

Publisher's Cataloging-in-Publication data

Taylor, Portia.

ˆBN-13: 978-1-64550-914-1

DEDICATION

This book is dedicated to my daughter, Paris Taylor and her entire generation. Have the AUDACITY to be who God called you to be.

You were born for such a time as this, now ROCK YOUR TIME! You are "Taylormade."

THIS IS NOT A READ THROUGH, THIS IS A WORK THROUGH.

CONTENTS

Introduction 7

Paralysis 13

Takers 53

Can You See Me? 89

Mind Your Business 105

Labels Are for Boxes 137

Challenge Accepted 145

Die Empty 159

INTRODUCTION

The Birthing Room

I remember being in the birthing room with Liz. This was her third child and while we were all excited about the birth of a new baby girl, we were also broken by the fact that she would never meet her father. He passed away suddenly and unexpectedly early in the pregnancy. Being the only family member permitted in the room for support, I was warned by the psychiatrist on staff that the trauma of his death could trigger emotions during the birthing process, and I needed to be there for her emotionally. I have walked with many women through emotional turbulence. I understand that while our emotions are a real part of who we are, they don't have to control us. We have authority over them. But when this day came, I too was flooded with emotions. With a lump in my throat and memories of such a great man, I gripped her hand as we prepared to push (yes, we). Everything she was instructed to do I would do too. We were in this together. *We* were having a baby today.

The room was cold, clean yet hollow, almost lifeless. Everything was sterile and quiet with the exception of the monitor beeping and the occasional moaning and grunting from mom. I knew that this quiet, clean and sterile place would soon be transformed because of the Pitocin hormone given to strengthen labor contractions and cause the uterus to contract.

She wasn't supposed to get the hormone. It wasn't in her birth plan. This was supposed to happen naturally, without any help, but Liz's body was more responsive to the trauma than the natural course of nature that her body was made for. She needed help to move this process along. After some time, the help kicked in and we were on our way to a new life.

As this room transformed, I quickly realized that the birthing room is nothing pretty. It was messy, even horrifying at times. The noises, the smells, the blood, the coaching from the doctors all were filling this room. They were shaping the environment baby girl would be born into. It all was preparing us for new life. I slowly glanced around the room while everyone was moving at record pace. A once orderly place seemed chaotic and loud. Things did not feel quite right. Fear showed up invited and I needed to locate him. He wasn't part of the birthing plan either. As my eyes continued to roam, there was a moment when Liz's and my eyes locked. I saw anguish in my dear friend's eyes. Fear was attempting to take up residence.

I knew this emotion was triggered by the trauma of losing her husband. I heard her thoughts. How am I going to raise another child alone? I wish he was here. Why did this happen? I don't want to be here. I can't do this. I heard it, looking in her eyes. Then came the tears of pain. I was empathetic and felt everything she was feeling. It was as if we were one. I decided to get closer to her.

I put my eyes so close to hers to show fear I was coming for him. I wanted him to see me. I became an intruder. Intruding, I saw something else. I saw something past the fear. I saw through her. I saw faith. She was laughing at fear. I saw her tomorrow, her strength. I saw beyond the moment. I saw everything else she was carrying that she needed to deliver for this baby girl.

When I got that glimpse, everyone in the room disappeared but her, and I became her midwife, her Pitocin. I would transfer the strength to her body that I saw in her spirit through words. "You were built for this," I told her. "Trauma cannot stop you or paralyze you if you don't allow it. I know you feel like giving up in this moment, but you have the ability to defy all natural odds. TAKE THE RISK!" I screamed. I got everyone's attention both in the natural and spirit realms. She looked at me puzzled. I told her, "Go ahead and abandon all those feelings that are overwhelming you at this time. You don't have to take on those feelings. Find some new ones!" I yelled.

Realizing I was causing concerns for the medical staff and it was just moments before they would probably call the psychiatrist on me, I tightened my lips and whispered forcefully, "Who are you? I am going to tell you who you are. You are the woman the enemy took his best shot at and still couldn't take you down. You are a woman of God with the strength of God. You are a mother, a queen, a leader. You are an overcomer—now have the AUDACITY to be who God has called you to be. Have the AUDACITY to tell fear to "kick rocks."

Have the AUDACITY to tell trauma you may have a piece of my past, but you will not define my future. Have the AUDACITY to thank God in this moment for new life, while still mourning the old one. Let AUDACITY through. It's disrespectful to what is supposed to be. It comes with an override button. It overrides negative emotions and crippling thoughts. Let AUDACITY drive.

Liz let out the loudest cry I've ever heard, repositioned herself and pushed in a way she had not before and out came our baby girl. I took a quick glance, but quickly looked back at Liz; she was laughing. She was overtaken with joy. I knew she was in pain, but the force of joy was much greater than any pain she could experience. As she held baby girl to her chest, she looked at me and said, "AUDACITY, that was the moment that evicted fear and gave me my life back."

Many of us find ourselves in environments and situations that hinder who we really are. There is seldom a perfect situation where we can bring forth who we really are. It appears messy and full of chaos. Or sometimes lifeless and hollow. We have to change our perspective on trouble.

2 Corinthians 4:17 New Living Translation (NLT)

For our present troubles are small and won't last very long. Yet they produce for us a glory that vastly outweighs them and will last forever!

You need to look at trouble as small and temporary. But also remind yourself that it will add to you, work for you and outweigh the problem. While God may not have authored the problem, He knows how to use it and FINISH IT!

Life's birthing room is messy to say the least. To be honest, to fight through all the thoughts, blood, sweat and tears seems frightening. But if I could get you to reposition yourself and focus on who you were made to be, you would have the audacity to come out with a roar. Let me warn you, as you read this book you will feel my eyelashes against yours, intruding on your made-up fears. You will feel me pushing the top of your belly, forcing that baby down. You will hear me scream and you may not like it.

I will force life into what seems like lifeless situations. It's ok. This is a life-giving book. It will raise situations, dreams and people from the dead. This book was not written for you to like me but for you to LOVE you. Christ endured the cross for the Joy that was set before him. That's YOU, sweetie, you are the JOY he died for. He risked everything. He abandoned every thought of quitting, so that you can live an abundant life, full of advantages. That same non-quitting seed that He conquered life's most difficult times with, now abides in you. That's right, you have non-quitting seed on the inside of you. So anytime you consider quitting on pushing, quitting on breathing, quitting on birthing, consider all He endured and name your baby Joy. It always comes after the trouble.

Let me re-introduce myself. I'm not the woman I used to be. I'm your midwife. This book wasn't meant to be pretty but to carry you through the frustrations of being overdue. To assist you with birthing in that uncomfortable position. To push and deliver your gift into what I like to call a beautiful mess. If you don't already know, I can talk loudly when I am preaching. Well ok, I do tend to yell. And when I am in deep conversations with folk I care about, I sometimes clap and grab the air to get my point across. There may even be a neck roll or two. Depending on the response I get, I may put my hands on you. But not in a violent way, I promise. Just a little push. You know the foot in the small of your back push. Some of us need it.

So while you read, imagine me doing every bit of that because I am. Imagine me invading your personal space, because I am. Imagine me intruding on everything average about you, because I am. Being a pastor, I often hear people say, "I was uncomfortable because I felt like you were telling my business while you were preaching." News flash: Where my readers are concerned there is no "my business." Your business is my business and I am in it and I am not just telling it, I am transforming it. Enjoy 😉.

Be Audacious!

P

CHAPTER ONE

Paralysis

pa·ral·y·sis

/pəˈraləsəs/

Feeling overwhelmed, stressed, anxious or fearful? Does it go away and then return like a cycle? These feelings can lead you to a state of paralysis. You lose your ability to move. You feel powerless. Or you may not feel anything. You have become numb. Are you numb in your relationships? When it comes to your future, your career? I've got good news. Well that's no surprise, I always have good news. There is treatment.

When doctors treat something, they typically are treating the symptoms in hopes that you will receive relief from the ailment or disease that is plaguing you. Most treatments are designed to make you comfortable. The thing about paralysis in most cases there is no relief because in many cases you cannot feel. There is physical therapy; there are exercises you can go through to regain feeling. Ultimately, they are trying to re-activate your circulatory system and get your blood moving again. Many times, you have lost your voluntary ability to move your muscles. It changes the make-up of your nervous tissue and results in metabolic disturbances that interfere with movement. Let me ask you, what has gotten on your "nerves" to the point where you can't move?

Treatment is good and it may give you a sense of relief from the pain, but you will be in a cycle most of your life treating symptoms. The best news is there is a cure. Which one do you want? I can tell you what God wants for you. Healthcare was one-third of Jesus' ministry. He didn't come to treat symptoms but to destroy the work of the enemy in your life. In 1 John 3:8 the Bible says, "He that committeth sin is of the devil; for the devil sinneth from the beginning. For this purpose, the Son of God was manifested, that he might destroy the works of the devil." The work that the writer is referring to is the work of sin. Sin has kept you bound for no absolute reason. It is Jesus' job to see exactly how you have been bound and tied up and untie you. Jesus' blood took care of sin. You need to break down that old blood and get a real transfusion. Applying His blood will get you moving again. Applying His blood against every situation that has you stuck will cause paralysis to let you go!

Jesus wants you whole. But I have learned something over my years on this Earth and dealing with His people. It takes courage to be made whole. Just ask the woman that *HAD* the issue of blood. We will talk with her later on. She could have continued with treatment that didn't last. She pursued the cure, but it took courage to do so. It took movement. It took her being able to receive. She repositioned herself with her back to her physicians and kneeled at the hem of His garment.

What position are you in? Are you standing up in pain or are you humbly kneeling, open for God to break you and cure you of every disease that came to rob and destroy you? Cures are realized when you break everything down and get to the root cause, not treat the symptoms. Wholeness is received when brokenness is released.

Before you read any further, I want you to answer these questions and get an honest answer from yourself. The word average is defined as typical and usual. How does that make you feel? Are you frustrated with the "usual" or "typical"? The word stuck is defined as unable to move, or set in a position, place or way of thinking. Are you irritated with the lack of progress or movement? Have you asked yourself if there is more?

The word fear is defined as an unpleasant emotion caused by the belief that someone or something is dangerous, likely to cause pain or a threat. Are you harassed by your own thoughts of danger or pain that could be inflicted on you? If the answer is yes, then you picked up the right book and after reading it you will no longer proceed to the action fiction books or movies where you will be inspired by a character possibly living the life that you only dream about living—escaping into their world for an hour or two weekly, get inspired, only to return to your world that lacks adventure because of fear. What about the supernatural movies with superheroes like Twilight or X-Men where you discover your superpowers or special gifts that empower you to move, see and feel beyond the natural. I bet when you watch them you resort to your childlike disposition and choose which character you are, don't you?

I can hear you now; "I'm Storm, I control the elements around me." Did you know that when you learn to tap into the power of Who is in you, you can control the environments around you? Or "I'm

Professor X, I possess superhuman mental powers." Do you realize that you can make your mind "mind" and through the power of your thought-life change your circumstances?

Maybe fictional superheroes aren't your thing. Is it the romantic novels or chick flicks that you place yourself in for an hour or two, imagining someone can love you the way you deserve, only to wake up in a passionless marriage where you are literally living with the equivalent of a roommate that you procreated with. You take one look at your spouse and see a lifeless marriage and decide to turn back on the television or open the book and fantasize about being someone else who is loved.

Or the single life with the nagging thought that you will never find the one you can't live without and you continue to settle for the one who will live with you without commitment? The empty promise of "I do" when you know they won't. And if you are really honest with yourself, you are only passionate about the "idea" of marriage, but you yourself already know what life with them looks like. Get out of that and make room for the real thing. Too far? Good, let's go further.

Are you done with living an average life without adventure, encounters and discomposure? Do you play it safe? Do you have more thoughts of something bad happening to you than something good? Are you tired of repeat conversations in your head about precautions and what if's or even worse, what will people think?

People Pleasing

Ah yes, the "what would people think" narrative is draining and overrated. The people pleasing is definitely an alternative version of yourself that cripples your ability to lead and increases your spheres of influence. I want you to pause right now if you deal with people pleasing. If you just had to ask yourself *Do I?* Chances are you do. I want you to make peace with the fact that someone will not like you, the decisions you make, your "nos" and even some of your "yeses." If you live for people's approval and affirmation, you will live in a lifetime of disappointment and self-sabotage.

Living a performance-based life is exhausting and downright dangerous to your emotional and physical health. Understand the world is filled with judgmental people who honestly don't like themselves, so they are committed to being a jerk to you. They will question your every move and make sure you know the potential consequences to every move you make. Let me also warn you not to make moves just to prove them wrong. When you live your life like that, you are living for them and not God. Living to prove someone wrong is bondage and drains you of your power. They have your power. You gave it to them when you made up your mind you had something to prove to them. You have nothing to prove; you are already approved by God.

Sometimes what we call fear of failure is actually fear of what other people may think. When people pleasing replaces God pleasing, fear of failure is at the root. Pleasing God must be our goal.

2 Corinthians 5:9 The Passion Translation (TPT)

So whether we live or die we make it our life's passion to live our lives pleasing to him.

If you take your wildest dream and act on it, see if your first thought is what would such and such think. The wrong people's opinions get you completely out of alignment with God.

God travels through our imagination. Even in the smallest and what may seem like your silliest thoughts, God is there. I remember dying my hair purple. I remember my first thought was I love the color purple; I want purple hair. My second thought—what will people think? Purple hair is out there. So, I told my stylist, "Don't make it too bright, too bold." That's so stupid. What is the point of making your hair purple if you aren't going to go bright and bold? Like there is a purple color that is not bright and bold.

I had to abandon those thoughts and reclaim my power. Purple makes me happy and at the time I wanted it in my hair. I rocked my purple hair. You should rock whatever makes you happy. I've since learned that God loves color. My purple hair was merely an expression of the God on the inside of me that wanted to get out. I was able to have many God-driven conversations off some purple hair. *Go figure.*

So, who cares what people think about you going back to school at 45 or buying a mini-van over an SUV because it fits your family's needs better? Stop giving weight to what people may think about your next move. You don't move and stay stuck because you have now lost you. The REAL you. The version of you, you are living out is one of everyone's opinions. Please turn off the people-pleasing frequency and align yourself with God.

Proverbs 29:25 Today's English Version (TEV)

It is a dangerous trap to be concerned with what others think of you, but if you trust the Lord you are safe.

How about asking the Lord what He thinks about your decision or next move? How about acknowledging *Him* in all your ways and not your girlfriends, parents, in-laws and the unsolicited opinions of the people in your life who don't have a vested interest in your outcomes.

Asking Him is so key to not pleasing people. He knows everything about you anyway. It reminds me of Adam in the Garden of Eden. Adam, knowing what God wanted, didn't say NO to Eve or the serpent. Why is it when we say no to something we feel as if we need to give an explanation? No is a complete sentence. Nothing needs to come before it or after it. You should try it sometime. Especially in the cases when you already have instruction from God, and someone wants to take you outside of His instructions.

Once you hear from God, boundaries are so vital. The enemy will always come with other suggestions and those suggestions will always be outside of the boundaries that God has for us. You remember the instruction to Adam was not to eat of the tree of good and evil. That was a boundary that the serpent challenged. Adam, probably in fear of not pleasing his wife, crossed that boundary. Once he did, he hid. These are all signs of people pleasing: 1) you don't know how to say no, 2) you cross boundaries for people, 3) you hide.

Here is the thing, you can never hide from God. Even when He asks, "Where are you?" It is for you to locate yourself. Hebrews 4:13 in the New Living Translation says, *Nothing in all creation is hidden from God. Everything is naked and exposed before his eyes, and he is the one to whom we are accountable.* If we live with the truth that nothing we do is hidden from God, and our ultimate accountability is to Him alone, we can live free of the burden of people pleasing.

Before you read any further, let me add a little balance to all my readers who see the world in black and white (all good or all bad, no gray areas). Getting the approval of others is not completely a bad thing. It just cannot be the main thing. It cannot dominate you. There is absolutely nothing wrong with wanting to please your spouse (PULEASSSEEEEE, please your spouse), your parents, etc.

What the enemy does is he causes you to think you are not enough or missing something, so the approval craving sets in and causes the desire to please to be unhealthy and rooted in lust or fear. There is nothing wrong with wanting to be loved. You just cannot give people the place in your life that only God should have.

God designed certain relationships to give us a level of security, affirmation and love and you too should be able to give it. If you are the type of person who always says you don't care about people, are typically numb when it comes to intimacy and affection where people are concerned, and you have absolutely no desire to please others, that is narcissistic and sociopathic behavior and you need to get delivered. This typically means you are self-centered and not Christ-centered.

Now if you read my last book, you know how I feel about friendships. God puts us in relationships for safety. He does things like gives you a pastor who can feed you with knowledge and understanding (Jeremiah 3:15). He does set up things in our lives well. You just need to know who you can go to for counsel. The Bible says in Proverbs 15:22 (TPT), *Your plans will fall apart right in front of you if you fail to get good advice. But if you first seek out multiple counselors, you'll watch your plans succeed.* You need *good* advice from counselors.

I personally call these people my board. Who can have a seat at your table? A board member focuses on what's best for the company or the organization or in this case, you. These people can speak to your strengths and weaknesses and can see how you see and many times further. These people should have experience, knowledge and most importantly, the ability to hear from God. Who is at your table? At the end of this chapter you will have the chance to write your list of counselors. It's important to determine who should be allowed to speak into your life. The right counsel from the proper relationships will make your plans succeed.

I was asked recently how do I personally define success? My answer was that I define success daily. I typically ask myself at the end of the day as I lay my head on my pillow, "Did I accomplish the will of God for my life today? Was He pleased"? And if my answer is yes, I call that a "W," a win. It's how I have learned to define success. When your desire to become successful is driven by approval of man, self-approval or trying to avoid being rejected, you are people-centered and self-centered. Instead, we must strive to be Christ-centered. Serving others is in our God-given DNA. We should serve. But when our motivation is to please man and not God we will come up feeling empty every time. Have the audacity to define success by what brings glory to God.

Colossians 3:23 TPT

Put your heart and soul into every activity you do, as though you are doing it for the Lord himself and not merely for others.

Because I know many leaders will read this book, I have to deal with people-pleasing leadership. This type of leadership will paralyze your influence and ultimately stunt the will of God for those who are under your leadership. Whether it's a church, your family, your staff at work, etc., we must be cautious in serving people. I use the word serving because if you are a leader, you should be serving people, not controlling or dominating them. That was a free nugget.

Galatians 1:10

For do I now persuade men, or God? Or do I seek to please men? For if I yet pleased men, I should not be the servant of Christ.

People-pleasing, approval-motivated leadership can be very subtle. It will rob you of your passion and joy, ultimately causing burn out or even worse, some type of moral failure. Don't be the leader who, when you have a difference of opinion, you don't speak up. When you know something else is heavy on you, but because you don't want to ruffle any feathers, you stay silent to keep peace.

If the definition of peace is nothing lacking and nothing missing, you are not keeping peace because your voice is lacking and missing. Speak up, give voice and lead the people. Sometimes being agreeable robs people of supernatural outcomes. As a leader, don't be afraid to push people with your voice. Speak up! Don't sacrifice it for counterfeit peace so you can look like you are non-combative and a sensible leader. Forget all that. Stop trying to look like something and BE something!

We cannot assume when others approve, God approves. That assumption is deception. Don't play to the crowd like Pilot did, knowing in his "knower" Jesus was innocent and found no fault in

Him, but the crowd wanted Him. Being a crowd pleaser he gave in and gave Jesus up. My advice? Don't give Jesus up for the crowd.

Luke 6:26 The Message (MSG)

There's trouble ahead when you live only for the approval of others, saying what flatters them, doing what indulges them. Popularity contests are not truth contests—look how many scoundrel preachers were approved by your ancestors! Your task is to be true, not popular.

Courageous Conversations

I realize that it takes courage to speak up. It takes courage to have hard conversations. My husband and I do a lot of counseling and whether it is in a marriage, with parents and children or between friends, we have learned that people have challenges with communication. We have further learned that we (collectively) were never really taught how to communicate properly. While we have all types of classes in school, I would like to propose a life skills class that deals with communication. I am not sure who is reading this that will accept my proposal, but I thought I would put it out there.

In the communication lab, Courageous Conversation, my husband and I teach people how to communicate hard truths without hurting your listener. Here is how:

Ephesians 4:15

But speaking the truth in love, may grow up into him in all things, which is the head, even Christ:

Here the Apostle Paul is making two commands to get a certain result.

1. Content-Your conversation must be truthful. Eliminate all lies from the conversation. Even the ones you are tempted to tell to avoid and appease your listener for fear you will be heard incorrectly. Many people say things they don't really mean in conflict and are inauthentic because of fear.

2. Method-Your conversation must be spoken out of love. It's the love of God that will cause you to share your heart. Your love for yourself and not being willing to hide anymore helps with this. But also, your love for your listener has to come through your language.

   As a result of the two commands Paul communicated, growth takes place. Our relationships will grow when we speak the truth in love. We become stuck in our relationships when we allow conflict in communication to overwhelm us. Don't be afraid to grow through communication.

   Speaking the truth in love is a delicate balance that must be practiced in conversation. Some people can speak from a place of love but forfeit truth for fear that the listener will become offended or not understand their heart. Or they err on the side of truth. They shoot straight from the hip with absolutely no love. They release verbal missiles. They are frank without mercy or tenderness. Truth without love is like surgery without anesthesia.

   To desire this balanced conversation is honor. Honor for

your relationships and God. We can't live our entire lives being horrible communicators.

I want you to ask yourself these few questions.

- What can't I talk about with my kids, spouse, friends, etc.?
- What causes me to explode?
- What causes me to be silent?

Once you answer those questions, I want you to identify one person you need to speak up and have a courageous conversation with them. Map out what you need to talk about. Write it down. Write *all* of it down. Then I want you to review the basic communication skills.

Basic Communication Skills in communication you must know what it means to be a good communicator (talker) and a good listener.

Good Talking

How do you articulate what's on your heart? It's not always what you say, but how you say it. Nonverbal communication is 63% of the conversation, so watch your body language when communicating. Your eyes, arms, neck and shoulders are all saying something to your listener.

A good communicator has clear articulation. Stay away from painting snowy pictures. You have to say what you mean in love without the fear of rejection. A good talker is honest and truthful. Again, don't say things you don't mean just to appease your listener. You sacrifice your own authenticity in the conversation. A good talker is tactful. Be kind no matter what the subject matter.

The saying, "Sticks and stones may break my bones, but words will never hurt me," is the biggest lie you were told as a kid. The Bible says in Proverbs 18:21 in The Message translation, "*Words kill, words give life; they're either poison or fruit—you choose.*" That tells us that words can wound, they can heal, they can build up and they can tear down, they can strengthen and encourage.

Good Listening

First understand that God gave us two ears and one mouth. What that tells us is it is more important to listen than to talk. Listening says "I care."

There is a difference between hearing and listening. Hearing is a function of the ear, while listening is an intellectual devotion to what is being said. It's very intentional.

I can remember traveling to New York City for the very first time. It was a work trip and my co-worker, and I stayed right in the middle of Manhattan. What an experience. Our first night there was restless for me. My co-worker, who is originally from New York, slept like a baby. I, on the other hand, was up all night. When she woke up the next morning and saw my restless posture, she asked me if I slept well.

"Sleep? Girl, no! All that noise all night..." I began to recap the night like a movie trailer. "There was a lady mugged at the end of the alley, three house fires, I think I witnessed a murder by gunshot and there had to be at least six break-ins between the hours of 1 a.m. and 5 a.m." How did I come up with all that? Because I was listening intently and carefully. I wasn't used to those types of sounds. My co-worker slept like a baby because she was familiar with the sound of New York. She was used to it. She heard with her ears, but she wasn't listening.

If you are ever going to get unstuck in your relationship with your spouse, your children, your friends, you need to listen. Stop hearing their voices like broken records and actually pay attention to what is being said. Stop being so familiar and anticipating what they are going to say to the point you are no longer listening. You are just hearing.

When listening to what someone is trying to communicate to you, your position is to listen to understand, not to respond. Responses have their place, but it's not *first* place, understanding is.

Proverbs 24:3 Amplified Bible, Classic Edition (AMPC)

Through skillful and godly Wisdom is a house (a life, a home, a family) built, and by understanding it is established [on a sound and good foundation],

A good listener listens to obtain understanding. You have to position yourself to hear your communicator's heart. You are not listening to agree, but to understand. A person knows that you are listening when you are not interrupting. You have to tell yourself in the moment that your response can wait, and if you forget it, it wasn't that important.

While your communicator is talking, beware of forming your own opinion. That will stop you from listening. While listening, be open. You have to understand that you don't know everything. You simply don't know what you don't know. You stop listening when you are judging, evaluating or assessing what is being said.

As the listener, the first thing you ought to do if you lack understanding of what was being said is ask questions. Questions bridge the gap. You can use phrases like, "What did you mean by that?" "Can you tell me more?" "Can you articulate why you feel like that?" If you ask questions, make sure you ask with empathy, not sarcastically. Sarcasm is a show of your own insecurity.

Now that you have gone over what it means to listen and talk well, I want you to set a time. Amos 3:3 in the AMPC version tells us that we must make appointments to communicate. We live in a busy society. Communicating "on the go" is unhealthy. Your relationships will not grow that way. Healthy things grow... If you are married, set a time to communicate, I like to call them communication dates. Time away to simply talk.

When having courageous conversations, sit congruent style, which represents being "all there." Sit eye to eye, knee to knee, hand to hand. Look at each other. Whether it is your spouse, a friend or your children, be all there. Allow the talker to get through the entire conversation without interruption.

As the listener, when they are done, it is important to repeat what you heard. Sometimes what you heard and what was said are two different things. Keep doing this until both parties agree that the listener understands what the talker communicated.

After that, ask any necessary questions you need to ask, then respond. You never want to end a courageous conversation on a negative note. Make sure every conversation you have starts and ends with something positive. It is called the sandwich method. I like to end with hopes and dreams. I like to say things like, "I sure can't wait until we go on vacation; I will get to hold your hand all day." It lightens the mood and leaves room for new possibilities.

So now that I have laid out a little instruction, speak up. (There is more, but you will have to get my soon-to-come book on communication.) Have the audacity to say it! Have the courageous conversation and be the best communicator you have ever heard!

Who Determines Your Success?

What about the thoughts of *What if it doesn't work? Any of it? Anything I set out to do.* I have a question, who determines that? Who determines your successes or what they look like? What measurements do you use? Other people? Please tell the truth. Do you get caught up in comparisons? Comparisons are so unproductive. You won't reproduce yourself like Genesis tells us to. You will reproduce someone else's self. That's called inauthentic.

We need to re-evaluate our wins in life. Sometimes you have to go back to the conception of an idea. What was the desired outcome? Did the work produce that or greater? Even if the process was hard and long, what was the fruit that was produced from it? Can you imagine if God after Adam and Eve failed in the garden gave up and said, "Welp, that didn't work, let's pack it up." God didn't look at that as failure. As if it didn't work. No, He always had a redemption plan in place.

His Son was always in the plan. His fruit was always you and me. He didn't give up because of what it looked like. He didn't stop at Adam and Eve. That didn't paralyze God and situations like that should not paralyze you either. I mean think about it… the Bible says consider Jesus who for the joy that was set before Him endured the cross. He didn't set His eyes on the cross but what was beyond the cross. You can't set your eyes on the hardship and what you may have to go through but what is on the other side. I don't care how many times you have fallen, *get'cha TAIL back up!*

Proverbs 24:16 NLT

The godly may trip seven times, but they will get up again. But one disaster is enough to overthrow the wicked.

Like my spiritual father, Apostle Tony Brazelton always says, "We don't fail, we regroup."

I've had times in my life when I dealt with paralysis. Situations paralyzed me. But I will tell you this, I never stayed there long. Circumstances cannot provide definition for me and the past can no longer hold me hostage. If you know me, you know I am a strong advocate for NEVER looking back. I remember feeling undervalued at my job. I prayed about seeking a new place of employment at a new level where I knew I could provide my expertise and grow. I got the release from the Lord and within weeks I was offered a new job. It was a promotion in responsibility and salary.

I put in my resignation to my supervisor that resulted in the owner of the company coming to see me. I said the OWNER, the CEO. I knew this was about to get interesting. He told me how valuable I was to the company and how they just could not lose me at that time. He then parted his lips to counteroffer what the other company had offered me. It was tempting. But I had an audacious thought: If you thought I was that valuable, why were you not offering me a promotion *before* I resigned. If I was worth that, why wasn't I making that.

Because I am a very honorable person, I kept my thoughts to myself. I don't believe in burning bridges. I simply replied with a *No thank you, it's time to MOVE FORWARD* and said my good-byes. You should add value to every place your foot steps. Don't allow anyone to devalue you. How much are you worth? Jesus would respond, my life. You are to die for.

Knowing God authored my life has kept me moving forward even through adversity. Adversity gives me fuel to drive me into new territory. Where my life is concerned, I know there is nothing wasted, and that God will use everything I travel through for my good.

I don't know if you have ever heard God speak to you right in the middle of what you called "hell." What He shows you seems impossible from where you stand, but you know if you simply trust and obey Him, there is something greater on the other side of this. In those times I would say to myself, *Portia, don't DIE wondering!* I'm too nosey not to see what's on the other side. I can't die now.

Some of you have died in your affliction. Not a physical death, but a spiritual one. You are walking around dead but haven't made it official yet. Don't be the dead man walking. Instead have the Audacity to live and live big. It is what Christ literally spilled His blood for. He didn't hang on that cross all those hours for you to allow your marriage or lack of resources to cause you to die. He didn't declare, "It is finished" for you to say, "I can't finish" and end your life prematurely. Don't die wondering what was on the other side. I refused and you should to.

I'm still the girl who on New Year's Eve of 1999, while the entire world was afraid of what 2000 would bring, was in great anticipation. People purchased all the water and batteries. Many thought the world was going to end. All the prophesies of the "Days of Noah" caused people to store up supplies in their "ark." But I was sitting there eagerly awaiting January 1, 2000.

I didn't store up anything because somehow, I knew whatever I needed for what was on the other side wasn't in my past. I wanted something new. I didn't care what was on the other side. Whatever it was, it had to be better. There were thoughts of a reset coming. Some feared it would take us into the Stone Age, but my expectation was everything that currently existed would end and opportunity for new life would begin.

Finally it was almost that time: 5...4...3...2...1...Happy New Year! Nothing changed. It all remained the same. They prepared for nothing. Where was the setback? There was none where I was concerned. When that clock struck signifying the beginning of a new year there was a new me. I had prepared differently. My expectation of God doing something new in my life literally prepared me for a new season. Nothing looked the same for me. My clock reset. I realized I didn't need water; *I* was the water. It was in me and in the right environment, it would flow right out of me. I was the ark God prepared to save His people. He invested Himself, the Savior, on the inside of me and He was coming for the return on his investment.

I didn't need anything from my past. I didn't need to look outside of myself for anything. It was my time and I was about to ROCK MY TIME! I stepped out the house the next day bold. Everyone was so cautious, they moved as if there were yellow yield signs. I ran, I built, I created, I took risks. I had lived to see a new decade. I felt like God was saying, *Portia, what are you going to do with 2000 and beyond? I created it for you to dominate.* I had my marching orders. Why am I alive now?

That day in an open vision I found myself standing right beside Jesus on a horizon. We were on the most beautiful beach I have ever seen. He was looking at something intently. You know I wanted to see.

John 8:23-24 MSG

Jesus said, 'You're tied down to the mundane; I'm in touch with what is beyond your horizons. You live in terms of what you see and touch. I'm living on other terms. I told you that you were missing God in all this. You're at a dead end. If you won't believe I am who I say I am, you're at the dead end of sins. You're missing God in your lives.'

Jesus said He is in touch with what is beyond our horizons. Which to me means He sees beyond today, beyond our circumstance and beyond what we can see. Listen in on my conversation with Him on the shore.

Jesus: Portia, as I look out beyond your horizons, I am happy that you took the risk, that you did not allow your present to keep you from all that I have for you. You were not made to be tied down to anything mundane. I love how anything that makes you feel hindered you get rid of it. You got that from me. I see you've discovered you have senses beyond your natural ones. Lead with those and you will always see what I see. So many miss the eternal, focusing on the temporary. I take pleasure in your audacity to be who you were created to be.

I enjoy it when you allow me to open doors for you. It brings me joy when you run through them. Most don't even see that the door is open. They stand at open doors. Some even sit and cry. Some pray at the door for me to open it or remove things in their path. They see that things are in the way. Can you tell them that those things are light? Just move them. They were not created to defeat or stop you. They can't. I even love you being here with me now. I wait here for many, but they don't show up. They don't make me a priority.

I giggled a little and said, "Yes, like buy water and store up batteries or even better, lay at an open door."

I giggled again because I crack myself up. He dropped a tear. "Oh. My bad, Jesus," I whispered.

Jesus: No, its fine. I love your humor. It's just that I ache. It hurts to see out on the horizon and to journey beyond the horizon to find very few there. I look back and they are still playing in sand on the shore. They are still trying to decide if it's God or not. They are still asking everyone's permission when I gave it to them at the words, IT IS FINISHED.

The shore was simply made for you to enjoy while you see what I have for you. The water is there for you to walk on. The horizon is just a mark to remind you there is something beyond it. Don't gaze at it like that's the goal. What's beyond it is your abundant life. Portia, what do you see?

Man, by this time my heart was aching too. Thinking about how we don't take risks because we think we will drown in the water or choke on the sand. Or how the horizon comes and goes, but God never leaves us. I was overwhelmed thinking about it and in that moment, I looked beyond the horizon and saw me. "Hey, there I am," I said to Jesus.

Jesus: Portia, what do you see?

"I see me in the water with a telescope and a flashlight inside a small tugboat. Actually, both me and my husband are in the boat. We have ropes and anchors. What are we doing?" As I looked closer, I saw us tugging at huge boats. Changing their courses. Leading them out for their journey. "Jesus, there are so many boats. But wait, what is all that in the water? Wait, are those people? I see us picking people up and putting them back in the boats. What's the meaning of all this, Jesus?"

Jesus: Portia, I created you and your husband to help people shift course. To get back on track. Many will jump ship, but you will have the tools to get them back on board. The tugboat represents your humility. It's so powerful and produces supernatural abilities. Your audacity to lead will impact fleets. It will not only change the narratives that people live by, to discover what in times past has been undiscoverable. They just couldn't see it. You will shine a light on new paths. Together your willingness to get way out beyond the horizon will open new waterways for others.

I saw a lot more that day on the shore with Jesus. Today I am living in what I saw. I want you to get on the shore with Him and answer the same question. What do you see?

Locating Yourself

If you are stuck, you certainly are not walking out on the water because it is impossible to be immobile on water. It is always moving. So, my guess is you are not using your faith. You are on land and probably playing with the sand because it is comfortable. It feels good in between your toes, but you cannot build anything on it. Not for long at least. As soon as the storms of life come, they will huff and puff and blow your house down.

Let's learn from God's first children. Read this passage of scripture in Genesis chapter 3, verses 7-10,

"And the eyes of them both were opened, and they knew that they were naked; and they sewed fig leaves together and made themselves aprons. And they heard the voice of the Lord God walking in the garden in the cool of the day: and Adam and his wife hid themselves from the presence of the Lord God amongst the trees of the garden. And the Lord God called unto Adam, and said unto him, 'Where art thou?' And he said, 'I heard thy voice in the garden, and I was afraid, because I was naked; and I hid myself.'"

During the fall of man Adam and Eve hid themselves in the garden. God asked them, "Where are you?" The creator of the Garden, He is all knowing. Come on, He is the God that sees and provides. But that question was not for God to locate them, but rather for them to locate themselves. Locating where you are is important to your movement. If you are hiding, you are identifying with the Adamic nature. That's not who you are supposed to identify with. Adam hides, Jesus reveals.

Where are you emotionally and spiritually? Where are your thoughts, especially about yourself? More importantly, why are you where you are? Why are you in the bed hiding under the covers

Netflix and chilling all the time? Why are you home making excuses when you should be on the stage, at a book signing, counseling, helping, serving, writing, singing, creating? God is looking for you.

The awesome thing about this story is He was walking in the cool of the day to fellowship with them. Even though they were hiding and out of position, they still heard God's voice. Wherever you find yourself in life, even in hiding you can still hear His voice. He still wants to fellowship with you. He just wants you to show yourself.

Wherever you are, it has you hiding.

They sewed together fig leaves, covered themselves up and then hid. Did you know hiding keeps you stuck? Especially if you feel you have done something wrong, full of shame. So you hide. I have learned that when you are full of shame or when you got mess going on in your life you don't want anyone to see, drag it into the light. Once it is in the light the enemy has no right to it. You get your power back.

Authenticity is always the best ministry. Be authentic. So what you messed up. So what you got embarrassed. So what it didn't work out like you told everyone. Have the audacity to get up and try again. Do it again like you meant to mess up the first time. Tell your story like it was always a part of the bigger plan for your life.

Many times people become paralyzed because they feel like their faith didn't work in a particular situation. They may have declared something publicly that never actualized. Or they experienced what they deemed failure or loss publicly. Can I tell you something? In the kingdom of God there is no such thing. If your faith didn't work, believe again. It just wasn't the end. There is no failure. It's called lessons learned or education. What did you learn from that? Apply it and go again. Lastly loss… there is nothing lost in the kingdom. It's just hidden. Just like you now. Be bold, step out and reveal yourself. God is waiting for you.

Steps to Getting Unstuck

You can read all of this and still do nothing. How do I know that? Because you have 66 books of instruction and still haven't done anything. I want to give you practical steps to curing paralysis, getting unstuck and moving.

Step 1: Don't Make Excuses

Excuses are monuments of nothingness. They build bridges to nowhere. Those who use these tools of incompetence are masters of nothingness. Therefore there are no excuses. –unknown

Self-awareness is so important to getting unstuck. You have to let go of the excuses that you have made monuments. An excuse is a false sense of security that makes us feel better about ourselves. It keeps us with low expectations of ourselves. Excuses turn into regret. I have resolved I will live a life of no regrets! If I have been successful in any area of my life it is because I let go of the excuses. Below are the top five excuses I often hear.

Excuse #1

I don't have the time to…

Truth:

You and the most successful person have the same amount of time. Lack of time will never be your problem. It's actually a lack of direction. Do not allow time to bully you. It is how you *manage* your time that counts. You will always find time for things you prioritize. Wake up earlier and write out your day. Be more intentional about how much time you spend planning. Declutter your life of unnecessary things and eliminate distractions like television and social media. Procrastination is the thief of time.

Excuse #2

I don't have any motivation right now.

Truth:

You are lazy. If you wait for motivation to come, you will never do anything. Get up and motivate yourself by setting attainable goals and creating new habits every day.

Excuse #3

I don't have what I need to…

Truth:

All you have currently is all you need to do what God has called you to do. He has already given you all things that pertain to life and Godliness. He has already supplied everything you need to be successful. You possess the faith for the grace that is on your life. You don't have to look far for anything. Just look inside.

Excuse #4

I don't know where to start.

Truth:

Pick a destination and begin. Once you get moving things will work themselves out around you. I personally like to start at the end. I like to spend time visualizing something complete and successful. Through that visualization, I tend to get the steps I need to take for completion.

Excuse #5

I don't know enough.

Truth:

I recently learned that "I don't know" is a spirit that keeps you in the dark. You have the Holy Spirit living on the inside of you and the scripture says you have an unction from the Holy One and you know all things (1 John 2:20). Rely on Him for revelation and commit to growth and development. Read some books. Listen to podcasts. Interview and learn from someone who is doing what you desire to do.

Step 2: Divine Focus

Having divine focus keeps you from being stuck. I said *Divine* focus because we can focus on many things, but I want you to focus on what God has said to you. Don't get over into areas you have no grace for. Stay in position and have the audacity to say no when you need to. You need to have an attitude like Nehemiah had when he was called to rebuild the walls of Jerusalem. His enemies tried many methods to stop the work. Let's look at some key statements he made in this story.

Nehemiah 6:1-3 MSG

When Sanballat, Tobiah, Geshem the Arab, and the rest of our enemies heard that I had rebuilt the wall and that there were no more breaks in it—even though I hadn't yet installed the gates—Sanballat and Geshem sent this message: 'Come and meet with us at Kephirim in the valley of Ono.' I knew they were scheming to hurt me so I sent messengers back with this: 'I'm doing a great work; I can't come down. Why should the work come to a standstill just so I can come down to see you?'

First of all, we cannot ignore that they were trying to trap him in a valley called "Ono," for me that is the first clue. It's literally called Oh, No! Duhhhh. He knew that it was a distraction. When you are building, you have to fight distractions. I love Nehemiah's response, *"I am doing a great work; I can't come down."*

You have to see your work as great. Don't come down from it. Stay focused. Stay high off of it. Allow your work to keep you "up" and call it great. That daycare you are starting, it's great. It's a lot of work to get all of your certifications and get up to code, but it's a great work. Don't come down. The work you are doing to stay free from addiction, yes, I know you have to go to recovery meetings and stay around the right people. Don't get lazy, don't come down. Stay up. There is an even more important part to this story. Let's keep reading.

Nehemiah 6:8-9 MSG

I sent him back this: "There's nothing to what you're saying. You've made it all up." They were trying to intimidate us into quitting. They thought, "They'll give up; they'll never finish it." I prayed, "Give me strength."

Know that the enemy will make up things to intimidate you. He will say things like, "*Quit because you won't finish anyway.*" But we need to take the lead from Nehemiah and pray, "Lord, give me strength."

While staying divinely focused, I want you to meditate on these two scriptures daily:

Psalm 119:1-8 MSG

You're blessed when you stay on course, walking steadily on the road revealed by GOD. You're blessed when you follow his directions, doing your best to find him. That's right—you don't go off on your own; you walk straight along the road he set. You, GOD, prescribed the right way to live; now you expect us to live it. Oh, that my steps might be steady, keeping to the course you set; Then I'd never have any regrets in comparing my life with your counsel. I thank you for speaking straight from your heart; I learn the pattern of your righteous ways. I'm going to do what you tell me to do; don't ever walk off and leave me.

There is a formula in this scripture:

1. Stay on course.
2. Let God reveal your road.
3. Don't go off on your own.
4. Don't live a life of regrets.
5. Just do what He tells you to do.

Psalm 119: 25-32 MSG

I'm feeling terrible—I couldn't feel worse! Get me on my feet again. You promised, remember? When I told my story, you responded; train me well in your deep wisdom. Help me understand these things inside and out so I can ponder your miracle-wonders. My sad life's dilapidated, a falling-down barn; build me up again by your Word. ***Barricade the road that goes Nowhere; grace me with your clear revelation. I choose the true road to Somewhere, I post your road signs at every curve and corner. I grasp and cling to whatever you tell me; GOD, don't let me down! I'll run the course you lay out for me if you'll just show me how. [emphasis added]***

My daily prayer is "Lord, barricade the road that goes nowhere!" Time is not something to waste. You cannot get it back. This is a powerful prayer.

When you are being cured of paralysis you have to give God your total attention.

Matthew 7:13-14 MSG

Don't look for shortcuts to God. The market is flooded with surefire, easygoing formulas for a successful life that can be practiced in your spare time. Don't fall for that stuff, even though crowds of people do. The way to life—to God!—is vigorous and requires total attention.

Jesus is the best example I can give you of someone who stayed divinely focused. I mean He was gangsta at 12. In Luke chapter 2 Jesus' parents took their annual journey to the Feast of Passover and when it was time to leave, they left Jesus behind. They thought He was somewhere in the crowd they were traveling with. This is why you should always be "watching" Jesus… LOL. These jokers journeyed an entire day before they realized they left Jesus in the temple. A whole entire day. Like you ain't check on Jesus to see if He ate *all day*? What about whether He used the bathroom? A whole day.

When they realized it, they went back to Jerusalem looking for Him. The next day, they found Him in the temple chilling with the teachers, listening to them and asking questions. The teachers were impressed with Him, but His parents were unimpressed.

Flustered, His mom asked Him why He did that to them. "We have been looking for you." Jesus' answer was priceless! He said, "*How have you sought me, don't you know I am about my Father's business?*" Now, most of us mothers envision Jesus on the floor after we slapped His mouth, but at 12 He knew His assignment and although not fully employed until 30, He was focused. He focused on the Word.

When you focus you will receive clarity. Jesus was always healing blind eyes. He doesn't like when we can't see. He doesn't like when we can half see. You remember when he asked the man in Mark chapter 8, "Can you see now?" The blind man answered, "*I see men as trees.*" That wasn't good enough for Jesus. He wanted him to see everything clearly. He also wants you to see everything clearly. This year will be a year of clarity for you. Don't stop looking, don't stop staring until you see clearly.

Step 3: Have the audacity to move forward.

Create space for something new. It's like cleaning out your closet for new clothes. It's ok to leave things and people behind that are not designed for your new space. Toxic people with toxic attitudes could not go with me. Things that reminded me of my past mistakes could not go with me. They are not meant to be in your next chapter.

If I am being honest, you don't know you are stuck in some areas or why you are even stuck. For many of us it has to be revealed. Past traumas keep us stuck. We think we have moved on when it really was simply swept under the rug so that we couldn't see it. Trauma is the response to a deeply distressing or disturbing event that overwhelms an individual's ability to cope, causes feelings of helplessness, diminishes their sense of self and their ability to feel the full range of emotions and experiences.

Trauma does not discriminate. It visits the houses of every creed and gender. Deliverance from trauma is not something we can deal with on the surface. You have to allow Holy Spirit to reveal the depth of the trauma. In order to move forward you have to have the audacity to abandon disappointment. Abandon self-pity and climb out of your pit. Negative emotions summon demonic activity. Don't linger in negative emotions. You invite influences in your life oftentimes unaware.

Many times, we need counseling and therapy to help bring to the surface any negative emotions trying to hide. Counseling to deal with the spiritual and soulish areas and then therapy to deal with the psychology. But in case you are ready right now, one of the greatest tools I used to help me, and others receive deliverance from trauma is *Self-Deliverance Made Simple* by Dennis and Jen Clark. It has tools you can use daily to get delivered and maintain that deliverance. Have the audacity to be free and be made whole!

If you are dealing with trauma, I want you to pray this prayer:

Dear Heavenly Father,

I come before you in the mighty name of Jesus; make your presence known to me this day. You are the God who is near to the broken-hearted and who cares and saves the crushed in spirit according to Psalm 34:18. In your name, I speak healing and restoration over every wound that was inflicted upon my life. I thank you for healing and binding up every wound. Expose every lie of the enemy that has entered my life because of trauma. Reveal your truth to me and let every lie be broken and every mindset come into alignment with the word of God.

According to Jeremiah 29:11 I declare your plans for me are good and not evil. I pray that you would help me embrace healing from past traumas. I ask you, Holy Spirit, to show me what happened in my life that has caused these negative emotions. I give you permission to dislodge memories that are stuck and keeping me stuck in areas not visible to me.

Lord, I pray that you would supernaturally remove the hurtful memories and the trauma of past events out of my mind, emotions, and out of my physical body. Lift all remnants of painful experiences and events and the trauma created as a result of that pain. I command my body to release all the effects of trauma. Lift it out of every cell in my body.

I forgive and release those who have treated me wrong. I forgive anyone who caused injury to my soul and even physically. I release hurtful words. I release all unforgiveness, anger, fear, rejection, pain and shame. I release myself and others from the pain of our past, and the poor decisions we've made as a result of our own brokenness. I release us all from guilt, shame, regret and bitterness now, in Jesus' name.

I give myself and them over to you, Father. I break agreement with the spirit of fear, depression, stress and anxiety. God, I thank you that you provide for all my spiritual and mental needs. I bind my mind to the mind of Christ. I bind every demonic force of negative emotions and replace it with the peace of God that surpasses all understanding. Disconnect me from every principality, power or ruler that has gained access to my life through traumatic events that I have suffered. I ask you to cancel the assignment of every demonic entity against me.

Lord, I call my soul back from any fragmented areas it has traveled. You said in your word that you would restore my soul. I thank you for making me whole and putting me back together again, spirit, soul and body. I command my body to release all the effects of trauma. I declare by your stripes I am healed. I am made whole.

Reveal your unfailing and everlasting love to me that casts out fear. Let your love reign down upon me bringing healing upon me. I release healing on my mind will and emotions. Overwhelm me with your loving presence. I declare only goodness and mercy can follow me all of the days of my life, and I will dwell in your house forever. In Jesus' name, amen.

You have to be willing to create new possibilities for your life. Have a meeting with guilt, laziness, frustration and disappointment and let them know you are divorcing them. Then give God praise and get excited about the new.

Have an expectation for the new. Most people don't expect anything because they are afraid of disappointment. You will miss God being afraid. God will meet you at your expectation. Allow God to breathe on those dry bones. "Pull for it." I often tell the crowd before I preach, "You can pull." When you have an expectation from God you can pull on the Holy Spirit, who will lead the speaker to speak right to your situation. Never underestimate the power of the "pull."

Most people don't expect anything because they are afraid of disappointment.

What will your next chapter look like? Imagine it, create it and walk in it.

Isaiah 43:18-19 NLT

But forget all that—it is nothing compared to what I am going to do. For I am about to do something new. See, I have already begun! Do you not see it? I will make a pathway through the wilderness. I will create rivers in the dry wasteland.

FORGET ALL THAT! Imagine me rolling my neck and clapping my hands. Let's go to work, He has already begun. I know you see it.

Here are some steps to move you forward:

- Break repeat patterns by breaking the cycles of repetition. You will break natural law. Don't do anything the same. Find new paths, go to new places, look at new things, have new experiences.

- Think new thoughts. I will deal with this more in the chapter,

"Mind Your Business."

- Develop new habits. Make a list of habits you need to have in order to move forward. Develop them daily.

- Spend time praying in the Spirit. He knows the mind of God. Push yourself to pray 30 minutes a day.

- Use your voice. Prophesy to dead things that should be alive. Speak to them. Prophecy reveals the future. Reveal your future now.

- Write the vision. I have learned through world-class motivator Terri Savelle Foy's sessions the importance of writing your obituary. This was a pivotal point in our lives. We sat down and wrote all that we accomplished individually and as a family. It cured us of paralysis. We started at the end, we realized who we were, and we let our past pass away and we moved forward.

It's time for you to move forward. Let's get to work!

Identify the things that have stopped progress in your life?

What have you been "treating" that needs to be cured? Think about repeat cycles in your life.

In what areas of your life do you "play it safe" and why?

Use the table below as a visual and place people on your board of life.

Wisdom is in the multitude of counsel.

Use the table below as a visual and place people on your board of life.

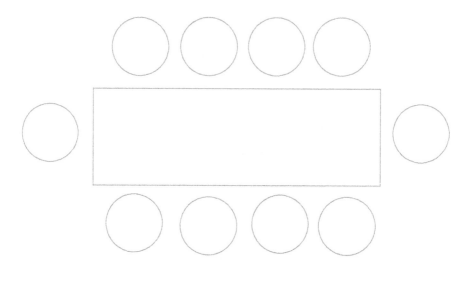

SEAT 1_________________________

SEAT 2_________________________

SEAT 3_________________________

SEAT 4_________________________

SEAT 5_________________________

SEAT 6_________________________

SEAT 7_________________________

SEAT 8_________________________

SEAT 9_________________________

SEAT 10________________________

People Pleasing

In what areas do you try to please people?

What people do you try to please the most and why?

Identify which types of people pleasing are healthy and which are unhealthy.

Courageous Conversation

List the people you need to set an appointment with and have a courageous conversation.

Before meeting with them, write down the truth you need to speak in love.

Ask yourself…

What can't I talk about?

What causes my explosions?

What causes me to become silent?

Don't make excuses:

List out your excuses. Once you list them draw a line through them and write the "truth" under it.

Example

Excuse #1

Truth

Divine Focus:

Spend time in prayer daily. Meditate on the scriptures provided and write down what God says to you.

Let's move forward.

Take some time and write your obituary. It will create space for new possibilities in your life. Start at the end and see how wonderful your life can be.

CHAPTER TWO

Takers

"Nothing important was ever achieved without someone taking a chance." -H. Jackson Brown Jr.

Pacing back and forth I wrestled. I could get into a lot of trouble. I could be arrested or even worse killed without anyone noticing. Girl, this is a risk, I kept telling myself. But I was at my end. I didn't know what else to do. No one had any answers, just criticism, stares and suggestions that I could not consider. I felt so judged.

I'm so tired. Tired of my environment, tired of hoping, tired of fighting but not too tired to save my daughter. Her episodes are getting worse. The things she says to me I know are not her. The places she ends up in are so deadly that I know someone else is leading her there. Another source, another power, she is demon possessed. Why my *child? Did I do something to deserve this?*

I will have an audience with Jesus. I will stop at nothing even if I have to sacrifice everything. So what I am not a Jew. I know it is dangerous to even approach Him, but I AM A MOTHER. I am her mother. It's time I stop fighting her and fight for her.

> I am her mother. It's time I stop fighting her and fight for her.

Here He comes; I run toward Him. "Lord, Son of David, have mercy on me! My daughter is demon-possessed and suffering terribly. He stares but not a word comes out of His mouth. I stare back. We are having a conversation with no words. I stare at Him intently, I see past His humanity and connect with His divinity. You know me, I say with my eyes. Before I was even formed in my mother's womb, you knew me. Remember me, God. C'mon, please remember me.

My shoulders rise up and down as I catch my breath from the run. The tears running down my face say I need you more than I need air. You know who I am, and I know who you are. In our moment of silence, the disciples urge Him to send me away, but our eyes are locked. To appease them He says, "I was sent only to the lost sheep of Israel." I step closer, knowing that at any minute I could lose my life. I would be ok with the loss because I refuse to live like this any longer. So, I drop to my knees at His feet.

"LORD, HELP ME," I cry. He speaks again. "It is not right to take the children's bread and toss it to dogs." For me, His words are not a no. Nope, they aren't a no. They are merely a response that provides an opportunity. See you heard, I am a dog. I heard, A crumb from Him is enough. My daughter was healed. I took her healing from leftovers.

I am the Canaanite Woman and the great faith I had to save my daughter was Audacious.

Take Your Seat

I was a government contracted meeting planner for over 10 years.

This career was high stress but a ball of fun. I formed lasting relationships, learned how to be flexible, think quick on my feet and most of all "fix." Yes, I became a fixer.

At this time in my career I was working on one of the highest level contracts I have ever worked on with government officials and notable members of the medical community. On this particular contract the meetings were small and secure. They met in hotel boardrooms that I contracted. The CEO of my company constantly stressed that while these meetings were small, they were the most important and yielded the most profit to the company.

I loved this contract because the subject matter was close to my heart. I had done a lot of research on my own and knew that one day I would contribute to the conversations at these highest levels.

The instructions in this contract for the setup of these rooms were detailed. I was to have a board table with only 8 seats. Each seat with a mic and a table tent that had each official's or doctor's name on it. I could only have 8 people around the perimeter. They were clear about which members of the press, executive assistants and consultants could sit around the perimeter. There was security at the door to ensure only the people who were supposed to be in the room were in the room.

As the meeting planner, I was responsible for all the logistics, but I myself was not allowed in the room once the meeting started. I was even instructed not to look some participants in their faces when they arrived. (I never agreed with that and broke that rule every time. That's not respect or humility; that's downplaying who I am.) I did have control over one seat at the table.

It was my responsibility to hire the transcriptionist who would transcribe. She got a seat at the table. Capturing what was said in that room and documenting it for years to come was important. Her job was probably the most important job, so she got a good seat. A seat where she could hear and see everything. A seat where she was also seen and heard.

My company won this contract at a turbulent time. We were threatened with the doors closing soon. We weren't winning any contracts and people were quitting left and right. Because I believed in the vision of the company, I hung in there. During that turbulent time I noticed my contract managers and other senior-level staff job searching and leaving for interviews. For me this was an opportunity. An opportunity for promotion. I made it my business to observe and learn everything I could about proposals, budgets and billing, contracting vendors and adding them to the scope of work, like the transcriptionist.

I have always been relational; I got to know everyone and spend time with everyone. My staff and I would do lunch together and sometimes hang out after work just to decompress. I hired this transcriptionist on a previous contract and had developed a special relationship with her because of her children.

I love to talk about family. I took a special interest in her children's daily activities and growth journey. In fact, this transcriptionist was only part time because her children were so busy, and she wanted to attend everything. She would only work a few hours a day because her family simply needed the money and couldn't afford to be a one-salary household. She was paid a weighty hourly rate to transcribe these meetings.

The day before one of these high-level meetings, I checked with all my vendors including my transcriptionist to ensure they had all the logistical information they needed to support the meeting the next day. We started at 8:00 a.m. sharp which meant anyone supporting needed to be there no later than 7:00 a.m.

It's 7:00 a.m. the day of the meeting and everyone was in place but my transcriptionist. It was not like her at all. I called leaving light messages like, *Hey, is Brian (child #2) giving you a hard time this morning?* and next, *How's traffic?* Gently nudging her. but then as the 8:00 hour was approaching, I was sweating. I was calling every five minutes, leaving panicky messages in my highest pitch voice. No responses. I looked at her seat and I looked away. I looked at her seat again and at everyone who was deemed important around the table. Everyone was there, but her.

It was time to close the door. That door seemed so thick and big at that moment. Right before my eyes it transformed into the doorway that would launch me into a new season. It was tight, but I was going to squeeze through it with my head held high like I belonged there. The seat that was empty and waiting for someone to sit in it looked like a throne. It began to light up as it grew larger. It was calling my name.

I grabbed a pen and pad and took my seat. (I know you expected me to say her seat, but it was occupied by me.) No one seemed to be bothered or even distracted by me claiming my seat but the board chair. She looked up at me and cracked her lips to say what would fuel me for the rest of my life. Who knew that six simple words would change the trajectory of my life? Those words would cause a stirring in my belly that I believe my boy Timothy experienced in 2 Timothy 1:6 when Paul commissioned him to stir up the gifts already inside of him.

The chair felt good. Like it was custom made for me. I was settling myself in it as she uttered those words out of her mouth, "You don't belong in that seat"!

YOU DON'T BELONG was a trigger for me. At that point in my life I was no longer allowing rejection to rob me of value. I was not in that seat to capture content but rather for context. There was something that only I could add to that table. Looking around there was no "me." Being seen and not heard was over. I was about to make all my ancestors proud.

I made a difference. I represented change. I encouraged new conversations, understanding that you simply don't know what you don't know. I listened and I challenged old models. It was so much more than taking a seat, it was taking a stand! Sure, the thought lingered in the back of my head, *I could be fired.* It didn't matter because I knew that day a prophesy was fulfilled. The one that said in history, *and she sat down and took her place and discovered who she really was.*

Much like in the book of Luke chapter 4 when Jesus walked into the temple, opened the scroll and found the place in Isaiah where it revealed who He was and what He was called to do. The scripture said it was fulfilled while the people were present and hearing, and then Jesus sat down. I love that. I can picture that so clearly because that was what happened to me that day.

I left that meeting on that fine day reciting the words of Ice Cube—Today was a good day.

That leap I took was a huge sacrifice. I could have lost my job that day. Somehow that thought could not stand up against my audacity to be who I knew I was. I also know I set a new tone for those who would come after me. For other young black professional females who feel unseen and unheard. For those who think because of their skin color, gender or lack of opportunity they will always live in support roles and be unfulfilled, knowing they have answers to and contributions that will last through our generations.

You are not living if you are not contributing. I have now learned if there is no seat at the table for you, build one. If there is no room, build an extension to the table, and if that doesn't work, go talk to Tyler Perry who made history by refusing to be discouraged at not having a seat at the table. He said forget the table, forget the room, I will build my own house altogether.

We hear names echoed throughout history like Sojourner Truth, Rosa Parks and Harriet Tubman, but do we really understand their sacrifices? They did not have the liberty of being distracted over a period of time or quitting because it got hard. Imagine the focus they had to have to complete their life's work. A work that affected generations. Do we understand the depth of love they had for humanity in order to continue in what would be the most challenging times of their lives? While we enjoy our current-day liberties and the freedom to be heard, have we ever had real encounters with that type of love?

My daughter did a book report on Helen Keller. Although blind and deaf she went to college, graduated with honors, traveled the world for a cause, wrote a book and learned three languages. She did not allow her disability to keep her in the dark and immobile.

She may have been in the dark, but she could see. She may have lived in complete silence, but she could hear. While most of us cannot begin to imagine being blind and deaf, what "disability" has hindered you from running your race and being an answer to the problems in humanity? Somehow after studying these women, procrastination, laziness and fear don't sound like disabilities anymore.

Recently while my husband and I were out of the country on vacation, I really began to think about this. Outside of the nice resorts, this country was poor. I began to ponder the liberties we have in our country, and how people died to give them to us. It led me to this thought, *Who am I 'dying' for? What am I sacrificing today so that my children will have a greater value for tomorrow? What do I love the most and am willing to give it up for the freedoms of those coming after me? What will I be remembered for? What do I fight for?*

Then I went even deeper. I thought about Isaac and what he witnessed when his father Abraham in Genesis chapter 22 put a knife to his throat, willing to sacrifice his own son out of obedience to God. It was a game changer. Isaac, not knowing he was the game, did not understand in that moment, but later did and was able to live from his father's sacrifice.

It then led me to these questions: What do we show our children about love and sacrifice beyond the occasional, "If it were not for me getting out here and going to work, you wouldn't have…"? What are they witnessing? What do they have a front row seat to? Love? Sacrifice? Honor? Or is it hoarding, complaining and fear? Have you ever done something that required sacrifice that did not benefit you?

What have we put a knife to with determination and no hesitation because of our dedication to something greater? In that moment, Abraham taught Isaac that there is no fear in love, but so did Rosa when she sat down without hesitation. So did Esther when she stood up for her people in the face of genocide. Those moments could have ended their lives but in both cases produced the life that we all now live.

We choose different times of the year to celebrate those who have gone on before us, but we should let them be our great "cloud of witnesses" all year. Many people died not ever being able to see the promise. Those things they laid down their lives for. On your journey, pull from their tenacity, courage and determination. They have gone on but have passed the baton and are cheering you on. Run with endurance this race that has been set before you. No matter what it looks like in the end, You Will Win.

Perseverance

As you journey through life you may face difficulty. Stop crying; that ain't new. And most things you go through someone else has already been through. You just have to have the audacity to get through and not get stuck in the "middle" of it. I do have some encouragement for you in the middle.

Perseverance defined is persistence in doing something despite difficulty or delay in achieving success.

Synonyms are tenacity, persistence, determination, resolve and resolution. The biblical definition of perseverance is endurance to stand fast. When there is resolution there is no wavering; there is staying power. You may lack the power to stay. Stop running all the time. Some of you run from church to church, job to job, and home to home. (Yup, I said it, take your tail home.)

You start something you know God told you to start, but when it gets a little tumultuous, you run and say it wasn't God. God didn't change His mind, you did! Have the audacity to stay and finish it. Some things won't be given to you. Some things you need to "take." The Bible refers to it as laying hold of something. Literally you have to snatch it and hold on to it with a death grip. When someone dies holding something it is almost impossible to get it out of their hand. Make it impossible for anyone or anything to take it from you once you have it.

God didn't change His mind, you did! Have the audacity to stay and finish it. Some things won't be given to you. Some things you need to "take."

Picture Jacob in Genesis chapter 32 grabbing that angel. He needed something from God before he returned home. He would have to face his brother Esau whom he betrayed. Like no, for real… he pretty much ruined his life and then rolled out and did not know whether his brother was going to try to kill him and his family. I love that instead of trying to build an army or even run, Jacob decided his best battle strategy was to get in the presence of God.

Earlier in a dream he saw angels ascending and descending from heaven with gifts from heaven to release on the Earth. While in God's presence Jacob sees an angel and grabs him, declaring, "I won't let you go until you bless me." He laid hold of something; he took something, and as a result, he obtained favor with his brother and had an encounter with God.

The Greek word for both endurance and patience is one word that means to bear up under. It means to withstand extreme adversity. These are the times you push through adversity. Whenever you have to push, understand there will be resistance. But you are not built to break. Let me prove it to you. Check out this scripture I found one day while facing an adverse situation that I was about to give up on.

Psalm 92:12

The righteous shall flourish like the palm tree: he shall grow like a cedar in Lebanon.

Here God compares the righteous (that's you and me) to a palm tree. This was such an intentional comparison. We are righteous people because of what Jesus did for us on the cross. The Bible says you were made righteous. There is nothing you did or could do to deserve it. God's people are unique, we may go through the same storms, but our outcomes are different.

Education on the Palm Tree

Palm trees were made to endure storms. You will notice that palm trees grow in climates with the worst storms, most of them living in tropical, subtropical and warm temperature climates.

I was meditating on the scripture just mentioned one day and decided to look up some of the worst storms in history. Guess what I found? Palm trees. I watched several hurricanes hit tropical areas. I saw trees falling all over the place. I saw the oak tree will break in half like a toothpick. That tree was no match for the storms. Pine trees that were over 100 feet tall were laying in yards, lifeless. I saw magnolias, elms, all down for the count. But not the palm tree.

The palm tree is designed to withstand the storm. There is a certain type of palm tree that can bend over until it is touching the ground and may stay that way for hours. It looks like it is going to break. While watching, I was thinking, *It's over, this tree is done* (LOL). *The hurricane looks like it is winning.* The bend in that palm tree made it appear it was broken. The palms were touching the ground. The tree was bending so bad it looked like something out of the matrix.

The hurricane was probably thinking, *I got you now, look at how far you are bending.* But I kept watching. There came an eerie silence. The storm had ceased; that palm tree was not dead. The palm tree had outlasted the storm. The hurricane was tired, but not the palm tree. As I kept looking at the palm tree bent over, looking half-dead, the palm tree stood right back up. The storm was over. The interesting thing is that when it stood back up, it was taller than it was in the beginning. It looked like it was taller than any other tree. Almost like it could see further than it could before, as if it had eyes.

I have learned that the palm tree is planted in those climates because it needs the storm to grow new roots and become stronger and taller. While the storm was raging, that palm tree was growing new roots, creating new possibilities under the ground that could not be seen by anyone.

Let's go deeper. Let me show you how storms work for you. Step outside of the storm with me and let me show you what is happening. When the storm is raging, its elements can make you think you are going to die, but what you may not see is that you are stronger than the storm. The storm is pushing you to a new place of prayer, worship and rest.

Instead of dying you begin to live from a new place. A place that realizes I am not built to break. This place unlocks the key to a greater depth of strength, courage and audacity in you that you didn't have access to before. C'mon, Somebody! God put bounce back in the palm tree and He put bounce back in you.

God put bounce back in the palm tree and He put bounce back in you.

According to Ephesians chapter 6, every believer will experience an "evil day," turbulence, a storm. When He created you, He made sure you had everything you need to withstand the storm. Yet, He also made sure every storm would not overtake you but cause you to grow.

I'm telling you, you need to have a moment like the main character in the movie *Antwone Fisher* and look in the face of your storm like he looked in the face of his abusers (they abused him mentally, physically and sexually). He shouted, "It don't matter what you tried to do, you couldn't destroy me! I'm still standing! I'm still strong! And I always will be."

2 Corinthians 4:17 NLT

For our present troubles are small and won't last very long. Yet they produce for us a glory that vastly outweighs them and will last forever!

Romans 8:28

And we know that all things work together for good to them that love God, to them who are the called according to his purpose.

I need you not to punk out. Not with scriptures like these. Sometimes we think when we go through things, we are going through them alone. We aren't ever alone. There are people who were here before you who fought the same battles and won! Some of them are mentioned in the Bible, some are your ancestors or even your elders. I like to call them my "cloud of witnesses."

> I need you not to punk out.

Witnesses have empathy, they have been in the game. They can offer a word of encouragement. Witnesses say, "Don't quit," "Don't stop." They have seen something; they were there before. That's why in the judicial system, there is witness protection. Those who are guilty are always trying to kill witnesses. It is proof that something happened.

Now be careful not to confuse witnesses with spectators. Spectators are those in the stands. They are just watching to see what's going to happen. Some may be cheerleaders or supporters, but some can be haters, waiting for you to fail. Be careful what you share with them. They have never walked your path. They haven't fought and won yet. Don't give them a place in your life they absolutely don't deserve. My spiritual mother, Apostle Cynthia Brazelton refers to it as "touching you" in her world-renowned message, "Who Touched Me." These spectators can look, but they cannot touch.

The Bible gives us proof of what is possible. Who are your witnesses?

Who's in your cloud. Let's look at the cloud of witnesses the Bible intentionally gives us.

Hebrews 12:1-3 TPT

As for us, we have all of these great witnesses who encircle us like clouds. So we must let go of every wound that has pierced us and the sin we so easily fall into. Then we will be able to run life's marathon race with passion and determination, for the path has been already marked out before us. We look away from the natural realm and we fasten our gaze onto Jesus who birthed faith within us and who leads us forward into faith's perfection. His example is this: Because his heart was focused on the joy of knowing that you would be his, he endured the agony of the cross and conquered its humiliation, and now sits exalted at the right hand of the throne of God! So consider carefully how Jesus faced such intense opposition from sinners who opposed their own souls, so that you won't become worn down and cave in under life's pressures.

In Hebrews chapter 11 we find that great hall of faith. I love the intentionality of who He chose.

Sara was chosen in case the devil punks you and tells you it is too late. What do you mean your time has passed? What do you mean you cannot produce? You've got a promise from God. The Bible says several times, "And it shall come to pass." The devil comes for your "shall be." Some of you have been waiting a long time for what He said would happen. Sara would tell you, it *will* happen. It may tarry, but wait for it!

Sara would tell you, it will happen. It may tarry, but wait for it!

Abraham is mentioned just in case God calls you out into a new place. He wants you to know that He is with you, even when nobody else is. Abraham had to leave his family and everything familiar to go to a place "that I will show you." Pause, so he had to pack up and just start moving without knowing where he was going? Like, what does that even look like? It looks like hearing and following the voice of God no matter what the cost. It's called faith. Abraham would tell you not to forfeit your destiny for comfortability.

Abraham would tell you not to forfeit your destiny for comfortability.

Noah would tell you that you can affect generations by obeying God. You can build an ark for your family. You can survive the floods. They are no match for your destiny! He would also tell you that it is never too late to begin again. Just kill it all and start over!

Enoch never knew or experienced death as we know it. He would tell you to keep walking until you are not what you started to be. You are changed as you go, you are translated as you move. He shows us that being immobile hinders us from the limitlessness we can have. He would ask you, How do you know this step won't translate you?

None of the people mentioned were perfect. Each of them had missteps and delays but finished what they started with audacity. There are more mentioned in the scripture. I think you should go and read the rest on your own and write down what each person is saying to you. It is called biblical application. Don't just read the story, *be* the story.

Don't just read the story, be the story.

Our journey with God is a marathon not a sprint. This is why you were built to last. In this marathon you have to drop some things as you run. The Bible warns us to lay aside the weights and sins that so easily beset us. I know when you read that scripture you think of things. It's the things that trip us up or slow us down easily. It's not always sins; it could be things that are just weighty, like wounds, offenses or bad relationships.

Have the audacity to drop it and let it go so that you can run your race. He wasn't the right one anyway. She was slowing down your pace with all her neediness and whining. You are focusing on the hurt and that has distorted your view of God's love. Drop it, him or her and take what belongs to you.

Opportunity and Discipline

Don't judge me, but I absolutely love the movie *Takers* starring Idris Elba, T.I., Michael Ealy, Paul Walker and Chris Brown. These men lived a luxurious life funded by bank robberies. What I loved about the movie was their ability to stick to a plan. They always had a blueprint with a strict set of rules.

What I further liked is that it always started with seeing an opportunity that the average person would have never seen. As a result, they were successful at "taking" until they got sloppy, until they allowed offenses from the past (T.I.) to join the crew. Like them, we have a blueprint; it's called the word of God and God always has a plan for our lives. But we cannot allow past offenses or a lack of motivation (laziness) stop us from taking everything that belongs to us.

I think the four men who let the paralytic man in through the roof can talk to us about seeing opportunity and taking what belongs to us. We can find them in Matthew 9:1-8, Mark 2:1-12, and Luke 5:17-26. This man was paralyzed. He could not move half his body. Jesus returns home to Capernaum and finds himself with a crowd gathered at his home. So many people that the four men that arrived with a paralytic could not get in the door. They didn't let the door or crowd stop them from receiving what they came for—healing for their friend. It is the perfect picture of community. I think they understood the picture of the body of Christ that Paul was trying to get over to us in 1 Corinthians.

1 Corinthians 12:26 New American Standard Bible (NASB)

And if one member suffers, all the members suffer with it;
if one member is honored, all the members rejoice with it.

Side note: You need some friends like this. Get you some.

Anyway, the Bible didn't say there was a hole in the roof. It says they *made* a hole in the roof. They saw a roof and somehow came up with, *We can get him in that way.* Do you think they thought about consequences or even *what if we drop him?* All of those thoughts are patterns of excuses. The roof provided opportunity for healing and they let him down through it. Look, this man was healed because of the four men's faith. The Bible never says that the paralytic said anything. It was their faith. Get you some friends that have enough faith to get you healed. This was creativity at its best.

Get you some friends that have enough faith to get you healed. This was creativity at its best.

You know someone else that saw an opportunity and took it? My girl Rahab. She was a prostitute who made the hall of faith. If you ever really want to have some hilarious, honest girl talk, talk to Rahab. She will tell you that God is no respecter of persons. He responds to faith!

I was willing to do whatever it took to save my household. I knew leaving my city would be hard. Jericho had been my home, but I heard that the God of the Israelites was about to do something big. Jericho now belonged to Him. I have given myself to many men, but I knew this God was about to be the one that I would give myself to forever. Until now, sex was my God. I served that God well. I was its slave in the worst ways. The payment was never enough. My service was never enough. I was so dissatisfied but could not see a way out, until now.

I wasn't going to be like Idit, Lot's wife in Sodom. I heard about her. I wasn't looking back. She lingered; I didn't hesitate. She held on to the old, I was about to leap into the new. Shoot, I already knew how to take something that didn't necessarily belong to me. I was a professional at it—sorry, ladies. We take much more from men than they think. A moment of pleasure turns into a lifetime of emptiness. Once he releases a piece of himself, he can't get it back. (It would take an act of God.) They won't admit it, but many men walk around feeling void, like something is missing. They keep trying to find it in dark places with people like me, not knowing that I was designed to keep taking and eventually my bed would lead them to their "hell" as Proverbs 6 mentions.

These days it looks different, but it's the strategy that gives women like I was the same results. These days they show up in DMs once he likes our pics on the 'gram, instead of lurking on corners.

Kings quickly become little boys in my bed, fulfilling every fantasy imaginable. They don't get that those fantasies are just counterfeit. The real vision God has for them is wrapped up in their seed, which I take. I take their ability to judge correctly, I take their influence, their leadership and while they think they got away with something with me, what they got away from was their future. It's forfeited when they sleep with me. They give, I take. I know how to take. But the new man in my life was about to fix all that.

My home was positioned perfectly for the situation and I saw opportunity. I always see opportunity. I am built like that, but Portia, so are you. Many people only see obstacles and challenges in tight situations. You can't just hide from it due to fear, you must stare at it. Many people look away too quickly. The trouble you ignore could very well be your path to freedom. My neighbors saw trouble, I saw life as I knew it was about to be over.

When I heard the news that they were coming to destroy the city, I had to find a way out. Joshua won nearly every battle and took more land than I have ever seen. I had no doubt our land was next. So, when he sent the spies, I hid them. You know I did. I've hidden many men in my home. I had the perfect hiding places. When the king came asking about the spies, I lied to protect them. I've lied for less and I somehow knew I was about to switch kings. He was no longer going to rule over me. His reign in my life was about to be over. It wasn't ending like this for me.

I had already given up a lot for little, very little (with raised eyebrows) and often I wondered if it was even worth it. Am I worth it? What is my worth?

The cord they gave me was my answer. It was a red scarlet cord to hang outside my door. They told me when the men saw it my life would be spared. That cord not only spared my life, it said to all men, she is taken already. I have never had that type of value or protection. The cord said, Don't touch her. That had never been said when referring to me. I didn't have to sleep with anyone for this cord. I've been touched so much I could no longer feel. But that cord, it touched me in places that I have never been touched. It unlocked places in me that I didn't have the key for. Portia, the cord was the key. Not just for me, but my entire family.

I've been touched so much I could no longer feel.

This cord saved my life. I left everything behind. I took nothing but a promise to be saved. Portia, this cord placed me in the blood line of Jesus. I got married. God gave me a man of my own. I married another taker, Joshua. Boy, were we a match. My acquaintance with my new King, my new God brought a new man. Girl, that man... whew, well that's for another time.

Because of my decision to take what was mine, Jesus came through my bloodline. My bloodline was cleansed, a prostitute, who thought she didn't matter. This showed me that God's grace accepts no boundaries.

Rahab

Isaiah 1:18

...though your sins may be like scarlet, they shall be as white as snow

Rahab reminds us that we are never too far gone for God to rescue us. He literally snatches us out of the hand of the enemy. She could have fainted in the midst of that, but she was strong.

Proverbs 24:10

If thou faint in the day of adversity, thy strength is small.

Faith revives you when you are about to faint. Faith takes. Be willing to take what is yours. Take your joy, take your peace, take your prosperity. Take it all by faith!

Stand your ground, don't you bow!

In adversity your position has to be, I will not be moved. The objective of the enemy will always be to get you to bow. Bowing comes before surrender and that should always be reserved for God. I am not bowing for and to no one. Jesus at his weakest point, after having fasted 40 days and 40 nights, was led into the wilderness to be tempted by the enemy.

The enemy tempted Him at His vulnerable points. He used food knowing Jesus was hungry. The enemy used power offering Jesus the "Kingdom," underestimating that Jesus would go through great pains to not only gain this "Kingdom" but to conquer the enemy's "kingdom" as well. Jesus would not bow. He stood on the word, which is solid ground. What I love about this story is that at Jesus' weakest point He is still stronger than the enemy. At your weakest points in life you are still stronger than the enemy.

At your weakest points in life you are still stronger than the enemy.

Matthew 4:1-11 Common English Bible (CEB)

Then the Spirit led Jesus up into the wilderness so that the devil might tempt him. After Jesus had fasted for forty days and forty nights, he was starving. The tempter came to him and said, "Since you are God's Son, command these stones to become bread." Jesus replied, "It's written, People won't live only by bread, but by every word spoken by God." After that the devil brought him into the holy city and stood him at the highest point of the temple. He said to him, "Since you are God's Son, throw yourself down; for it is written, I will command my angels concerning you, and they will take you up in their hands so that you won't hit your foot on a stone. " Jesus replied, "Again it's written, Don't test the Lord your God." Then the devil brought him to a very high mountain and showed him all the kingdoms of the world and their glory. He said, "I'll give you all these if you bow down and worship me." Jesus responded, "Go away, Satan, because it's written, You will worship the Lord your God and serve only him." The devil left him, and angels came and took care of him.

Let's look at the three Hebrew boys.

Daniel 3:1-7New King James Version (NKJV)

Nebuchadnezzar the king made an image of gold, whose height was sixty cubits and its width six cubits. He set it up in the plain of Dura, in the province of Babylon. And King Nebuchadnezzar sent word to gather together the satraps, the administrators, the governors, the counselors, the treasurers, the judges, the magistrates, and all the officials of the provinces, to come to the dedication of the image which King Nebuchadnezzar had set up. So the satraps, the administrators, the governors, the counselors, the treasurers, the judges, the magistrates, and all the officials of the provinces gathered together for the dedication of the image that King Nebuchadnezzar had set up; and they stood before the image that Nebuchadnezzar had set up. Then a herald cried aloud: "To you it is commanded, O peoples, nations, and languages, that at the time you hear the sound of the horn, flute, harp, lyre, and psaltery, in symphony with all kinds of music, you shall fall down and worship the gold image that King Nebuchadnezzar has set up; and whoever does not fall down and worship shall be cast immediately into the midst of a burning fiery furnace." So at that time, when all the people heard the sound of the horn, flute, harp, and lyre, in symphony with all kinds of music, all the people, nations, and languages fell down and worshiped the gold image which King Nebuchadnezzar had set up.

These three Hebrew boys found in Daniel chapter 3 refused the king's culture and would not bow down to anything that caused them to be put in the furnace. It really speaks of Identity. They would not bow down to the king's false *image*. Do not bow down to false images of yourself or even the atmosphere that this culture tries to set. In this story music was used. The king said, "When you hear the music, you must bow down and worship. Satan will always try to use your gates of life to access your heart. Here, he uses the ear gate. He still does it today. What sounds are you hearing that cause you to bow? Identify them now. You cannot wait until you are in the furnace before you decide you will not bow down. You may be put in the furnace, but your decision must already be made. Please know God is the ultimate man of fire and will stand with you in the furnace.

Do you realize when you are with God, *nothing* can take you out? He never promises things won't happen. In this world there will be trouble. But then He says, but don't sweat trouble because He has overcome this world (John 16:33). That's why you can't keep company with people who live and talk defeat all the time. God paid the ultimate price to keep company with you. With Him, you can get through anything!

Do you realize when you are with God, nothing can take you out?

Isaiah 43:1-2 NKJV

But now, thus says the LORD, who created you, O Jacob, And He who formed you, O Israel: "Fear not, for I have redeemed you; I have called you by your name; You are Mine. When you pass through the waters, I will be with you; And through the rivers, they shall not overflow you. When you walk through the fire, you shall not be burned, Nor shall the flame scorch you.

Permission Granted

A great picture of this was in John chapter 5 with the lame man by the pool. In verse 7 he told Jesus that "no man" could put him in the pool when it was stirred. Now *that* was lame. It was a lame excuse. I can imagine Jesus saying, "You have been this way for 38 years and you have been waiting on a *man*." You are blaming a *man*. You trying to tell me in 38 years you could not figure out how to get in the pool? You could have rolled a little every day for 13,870 days. Ok, Jesus may not have said or thought that, but I sure did. In all that time, you could have come up with a strategy to get in that pool.

Blaming comes from a victim mentality. It produces hopelessness. It lies to you and tells you there is nothing you can do. Well here is what I want you to do right now. I want you to think about the lame man's bed and then think about your own bed. Most of our beds are comfortable. We even have comforters on our beds that we love. Jesus' instruction to the lame man was to pick up his bed and walk. I want you to start to pick up what you have been lying in. Throw off what you are wrapped in that's got you snug and comfortable. I need you to come up with a strategy to WALK! For this man, it was the release of word out of Jesus' mouth. Well you have 66 books of words from heaven. Put them in your own mouth and let's get moving.

Blaming comes from a victim mentality.

John 5:8 English Standard Version (ESV)

Jesus said to him, "Get up, take up your bed, and walk."

Why do we wait for someone's permission to be who God called us to be? Really, answer that for yourself, why? Outside of the spiritual authorities in your life that may need to release a blessing over you, who are we looking for to validate us? Who needs to affirm us before we can step into what God has for us?

Sure sometimes there is someone there to push you, like Esther's uncle Mordecai did her when her people were facing death. He had to remind her who she was. He had to remind her that she came from those people and the enemy was coming for them. He had to remind her that she was positioned correctly by God for such a time as this. Sounds like Rahab, doesn't it? I promise you, when you find out who you really are you will realize, we are all connected.

Is that it? Do we simply need to be reminded who we are in order to move out into what we are called to do? Well let me take a moment to remind you: You are fearless, flawless, bold and courageous. You are equipped with everything you need to win in this life. You are a barrier breaker, a bridge, an agent of change. You carry deliverance for humanity in your belly. You are Jesus' representative in the Earth, and He didn't need permission. He was straight up about His father's business.

You are fearless, flawless, bold and courageous. You are equipped with everything you need to win in this life.

Leadership is a part of the human experience; you are a leader. You possess the wisdom and strength you need to overthrow, to root out, to build and to plant. You were ordained before you were formed in your mama's womb. Stop waiting for man to ordain you. You don't need the papers; everything you need is already written, signed, sealed and stamped by your Father.

Stop asking who you are and *be* who you are. What would happen if you stopped asking permission and just did it? Grow up. Grown folk don't ask permission. Don't ask this world nothing. The darkness in this world wasn't designed to provide you with answers. Live from a different world. Live from the realities of heaven.

2 Corinthians 1:20 NLT

For all of God's promises have been fulfilled in Christ with a resounding "Yes!" And through Christ, our "Amen" (which means "Yes") ascends to God for his glory.

Let's talk to the woman with the issue of blood. She sure didn't ask anyone's permission.

Portia: Hey, look at you all healed and stuff. Standing straight up.

Woman: [Chuckles] Yes, look at me, but you know I was bent over for so long, sometimes I have to remember that I am healed and walk like it. It takes courage to be made whole. It provides a new life where you are no longer the victim. Portia, people aren't whole because they like being the victim. They like the attention it brings. They like the fact they are dependent on others to do things for them. It provides excuses as to why they can't get things done. Living whole requires a mindset shift. Sometimes the handicap isn't in your body, it's in your mind. I lived in isolation so long that I had to learn how to enjoy people and life.

Portia: When I read about you, I am always impressed by your tenacity and perseverance to get through that crowd to touch Jesus.

Woman: Impressed? *Pshht*, girl I risked my life that day to touch Him. I didn't care not one bit about the consequence. Do you know what it's like to be broke and sick, living as a defiled woman? No husband or children for me in sight? No friends or family? Every chair I sat in, every cup I touched, considered defiled because of my "lil sister" wanting to act up daily. You don't know the rejection I faced daily or shoot, how many times I had to wash my clothes. There was disjointedness due to loneliness. Something so private becoming something so public. I was ashamed. They put shame on me. *I* put shame on me. Twelve years of this was a lifetime and I was going to take my life back. If what I heard about this Man was true, I wasn't going to let any man out there stop me that day. I had a fight in me.

Portia: Talk about that moment, that touch. What did it feel like, virtue leaving Him, you being healed?

Woman: Healed? I was made whole. That touch changed everything. You know, Portia, I remember crawling on the ground and keeping my eyes on His robe. I was already so broken, I didn't care if I was stepped on or trampled, kicked or beaten. There was nothing worse than living like I was living. I always felt so miserable, tired, worn, just all over the place. So, when I said, "If I could just touch the hem of his garment I will be made whole," I felt something starting to happen. But not in my body yet, in my mind.

My declaration caused an acceleration, and before I knew it, I was there at the hem of His garment and once I actually touched Him, the warmth, the sensation I felt, I immediately knew I was healed. But the wholeness didn't come at that moment. No, it was when He spoke. It wasn't until He said, "Daughter." (Her voice cracking and tears rolling down her face.) It was like I always knew Him. Like I was lost, but now reunited with my Father. I touched divinity and He touched my purity. The little girl in me leaped.

It was the acceptance from Jesus. Those words caused me to get off my knees and look in His face. I saw my Father. He saw me. The real me. That feeling of wholeness is indescribable, Portia. Those twelve years bent over could not stand up to this moment.

That moment murdered rejection and concealed loneliness. Staring at him I felt cradled and secure. "Daughter, thy faith has made you whole." I was healed when I cried out, but wholeness came from my Father's touch of acceptance. Shame off me, I will never forget it. I chased Him down for what He could do, I was accepted because of who He was, my Father.

My conversation with this woman was impactful in my life. One thing I realized was through her entire story she never said she asked to see Jesus. She didn't ask his disciples or any of the guards or religious rulers of that day. She pressed and dropped and finally reached out without anyone's permission. Her wholeness didn't require anyone's permission. She didn't wait to see if the conditions were favorable to take what belonged to her. She was tired and said, It's time for me!

Self-Care

Many times our bodies can act up and do prolonged weird things because we are simply tired. We go to work, school, church, wherever—bent over. We just keep moving and sometimes our Father just wants us to stop and look in His face. It's called self-care. It's called taking care of this temple He gave us. We don't need anyone's permission to do that. Not our children's, our spouse's, our boss', no one's.

We need to know when we need to take a moment for ourselves. I kind of learned that the hard way. Y'all know I have many funny stories, well let me tell you about the "carpool line."

It was an absolutely beautiful day. It was early spring, just enough chill to feel that amazing breeze hit your face, but just enough warmth where you didn't need a jacket. I got to my daughter's school early because I was exhausted and my thought was, *Let me go early, so I can be first in line, get Paris and get home quickly to start dinner, help with homework and maybe get in bed early.* There were no evening services, no meetings, nothing. That's a thought, go to bed early.

I pulled up to the carpool, *Yes, I am the first one here.* The carpool was two lines side by side and I pulled to the left lane. There were teachers' aides there to control traffic, letting you know when you could pull forward and extract your child. Most parents know that the carpool line is a big deal. Stay in the cones, keep your car running, pull up quickly, get that child in the car and pull off because the line is ridiculously long.

First one, it's 2:50. I have 10 minutes before the start of the car line pick up. I went ahead and turned off the car (knowing that is against the rules, but hey, I had some time). I slightly rolled down my window and that breeze hit just right. *Ahhh, feels so good.* I turned my body slightly to the right and got into the fetal position as I reclined my chair. *Let me close my eyes for a few moments*, I thought.

Bang, Bang, Bang, the startling sound of eight police officers knocking is what I woke up to. "Mrs. Taylor!" she screamed. Mrs. Taylor *they* screamed. It was 3:08 and the car line had been mobile for eight minutes while I was asleep. In a deep sleep, mouth open and drooling, I think I was dreaming sleep. I was startled. I looked up and turned my car on, rolled down my window, saying I was sorry. But the teachers were laughing so hard as they were redirecting traffic around me and the line for carpool was now backed up into the highway because of my need for "eight minutes." (I actually think one of the teachers peed herself from laughing so hard.)

As I pulled forward, embarrassed and not even wanting to look my child in her face, one intrusive, yet caring teacher leaned in and said, "Honey, you need to slow down and take care of yourself. Ain't nothing that important that you need to lose sleep for, and please, next time just park and walk up because carpool line is not for you." I won't share the thoughts I had for her in my head that I did not allow to come out of my mouth. I responded with a calm, "Thank you," and "No, I prefer the carpool line. I will do better."

I learned that day the importance of taking time for yourself. You don't need anybody's permission to take a nap. *Take it.* Just don't do it during carpool. Take time for yourself. This was a process for me.

"When you say yes to others make sure you are not saying no to yourself."-Unknown

Still learning self-care, one Saturday I opened my eyes and I realized I had a day. *One day* where there were no appointments, no work, no meetings, no cleaning the house (Well, I am sure there was some cleaning to be done, but I did not *have* to do it.), no speaking engagement or classes to teach, *nothing*. Hubby was out of town traveling and Paris had a playdate; that left me home alone.

As I rolled myself out of bed, I had a thought, *I could really use some retail therapy.* I love shopping. I am not a group shopper. I am not one to go out to the mall with the girls all day and window shop. While I will do that for my girls, I prefer to shop alone. I talk to myself, talk to the Lord, cry when it doesn't fit and dance when it does. But at this time in my life, I had not been out, nor had I done anything for myself in a long time. I could not even remember the last time I had shopped or even gotten a pedicure.

This was the day. But even as I got out of bed to get in the shower, I was so tired. I was cloudy and had a slight headache, the kind that comes from not getting enough rest. I chose a mall far away because I really wanted a good drive and some "me" time. When

I arrived at the mall, I did as I always do, I took one lap around to all my favorite stores, glanced around, and then I would normally return to actually purchase things I saw.

I went into one store and decided I am going to try everything on I want; after all, I have the entire day. I chose about five tops and four bottoms. I went in the dressing room and began to undress while I freely sang and danced like nobody was watching (you should try it). I put on the first top. It was cute. *Let's see what pants can go with this.* I put on some high-waisted slacks and they were cute. I was twirling, having a great time and then the phone rang. It was like the power going out while watching your favorite movie. Someone needed me and they needed me right then.

My response: "Ok, I am coming." My mind started racing. How long will it take me to get to them? Where did I park? Where are my keys...ugggg!? Where are my clothes? I ripped off the cute shirt, put my original shirt on, took off those cute high-waisted pants. There was no time to buy those now. Put on my tennis shoes, threw my purse over my shoulder and headed out of the dressing room.

Right before I approached the doors to the general public area of the store, I felt a draft. I look at the dressing room lady as she looked at me confused. I looked down...*I don't have any pants on!* Just drawls and a top with my purse like a crack smoker on 14th street!

Self-care is not selfish; it is good stewardship of the only thing God put you on the Earth with—yourself.

Self-care is not selfish; it is good stewardship of the only thing God put you on the Earth with—*yourself.* I believe one of the hardest lessons I have had to learn in life, and am still learning, is how important it is to care for yourself *first.* Sometimes even saying that makes me feel a bit guilty. That feeling comes from a very unrighteous place and I resist it daily.

You have to take care of yourself first (second to God), in order to be healthy and show up for others spiritually, emotionally, intellectually and physically. It is not egocentric or selfish. You cannot give away what you don't have.

Most overly-occupied people don't even know what they like anymore. They can't tell you their favorite color, what great book they've read lately, or what their primary hobby is. I think there are habits we developed in grade school that we should have never let slip. Like nap time and time out. Sometimes you need a time out. Time to sit and meditate on what you did. What you are doing. Where you are going and REST. Rest is a commandment that God put in place. Everyone needs a Sabbath.

One of the greatest pictures of this is the story of Mary and Martha in the Bible. Mary understood this, but Martha struggled with it. Martha was overly occupied and too busy while Mary sat at the feet of Jesus. I love that Mary had the audacity to tell Martha no. What Martha was doing seemed like something that should have been done, but it wasn't the needful thing at the time.

I struggle with the Mary and Martha inside of me. Holy Spirit helped me to discover who gets the front seat and when. I learned sometimes we are trying to serve Jesus doing something He doesn't want at that time. Sometimes He wants you at His feet.

Sitting at the feet of Jesus is the highest form of self-care there is. When He is your priority everything else will align properly. I now know that. Do something different today. Sit in time out, take a nap and don't forget to put your pants on.

Sitting at the feet of Jesus is the highest form of self-care there is.

Let's do the work.

Who is in YOUR cloud?

What do you need to lay aside in order to run? LET IT GO!

What things in life do you need to finish?

Jacob grabbed onto an angel. What do you need to grab?

Identify the comfy beds in your life. Then take them up and walk.

Who do you tend to ask permission from and why?

Write down some confessions to remind yourself daily who you are.

Spend some time in prayer and write down some kingdom strategies that will get you to take up your bed and walk.

Look at your calendar for the week and plan some self-care time. Write it below.

CHAPTER THREE

Can You See Me?

"Insignificance Is A Lie!"-Portia Taylor

I was a youth leader attending a youth group function at someone's home. Generally, I have a really hard time using the bathroom outside my home. I literally have to talk myself into it. Well this was a time that I just could not "hold it." We were all gathered in the family room looking at something on the television screen. The bathroom happened to be behind everyone in between the kitchen and the basement door.

As I dashed for the bathroom there were two doors backed up against one another. The wooden bathroom door and the glass French basement door. As I went into the bathroom, I shut the door. I began to get in position for that amazing squat I have mastered because I am not sitting down, I look up to ease my mind, maybe thinking there would be some fabulous artwork on the walls, and to my surprise I SEE PEOPLE. I see the back of the heads of all the youth and before I could question in my head WHY can I see them, I get a quick glance from my sister who was also there but facing me.

I look at her and mouth while pointing my index finger to my chest, *"CAN YOU SEE ME?"* I was beyond puzzled. Her response, "*YES FOOL, I CAN SEE YOU. WHAT ARE YOU DOING?*" I then realized that somehow, I had closed the wrong door. I had closed the glass door instead. Gasping for air as I was laughing so hard, I quickly pulled up my pants (Somehow the urge left, maybe I "let it go" laughing.), and joined the rest of the group. My sister gave me the side-eye the entire rest of the event.

Another one of my favorite movies is *Freedom Writers.* Erin Gruwell, played by Hilary Swank is a dedicated teacher in a racially divided Los Angeles school. She dedicated her entire life to helping at-risk teenagers deemed incapable of learning. Through hard times for both her, personally, and the kids she is successful at getting to see they are more than where they came from. In a compelling scene, she addressed one of her students, Andre Bryant played by Mario, a now upstanding student, who had just seen his brother be sentenced to jail. He suddenly stopped coming to school, and looked as if he was giving up by getting a "F" on an assignment. "I SEE YOU!" Mrs. Gruwell said to him. She shut the door before he could get into the classroom.

What she was saying was despite the exterior brick wall you are giving me and lack of effort coming from you right now—I SEE YOU. The real you. The vulnerable, unclothed, uncovered you. Despite your momentary desire to give up due to the current events in your life—I SEE YOU. I see your end. I see you graduating not only from high school but college. I SEE YOU being an upstanding citizen, raising a family, contributing greatly to society. I SEE beyond today.

While it was just a movie, I know how Andre felt in that moment. It was a moment of impact that would change his life. I know, I experienced it myself in the 10th grade. Running down the hallway late to my black history class at Seneca Valley High School (GO EAGLES).

I was always late to that class, but this time as I approached the door it slammed and Ms. Wilson my teacher, my "Mrs. Gruwell" stepped outside, got in my face and asked, "How many times are you going to be late? These teachers and administrators expect for YOU to be loud and late, but not me. I SEE YOU. I know who you really are and what you can really accomplish." She got even closer where I felt like our eyelashes were touching and she said, "SURPRISE SOMEBODY! Do something different for a change; BE who you really are, not who you are pretending to be."

BE who you really are, not who you are pretending to be.

As adults we may no longer have the Ms. Wilsons and Erin Gruwells in our lives, but we need them. Once I got my act together, I promised myself that I would always be that for someone. And TODAY it's for you, my reader. I want you to know I SEE YOU. Although you may feel like no one does and you are a mess, that mess is not who you are.

Although you are producing F's in life right now, I know you've got A's in you. You have allowed life to bully you, but I am here to bully that bully and remind you that you are like no other. You are great. I see you starting. I see you finishing. I see your imprint in life, it's unique. Yes, for a moment you may have forgotten who you are, but I am here to remind you that the ONE that created you carefully watches you.

Psalm 121:5-8 New International Version (NIV)

The Lord himself watches over you! The Lord stands beside you as your protective shade. The sun will not harm you by day, nor the moon at night. The Lord keeps you from all harm and watches over your life. The Lord keeps watch over you as you come and go, both now and forever.

HE SEES YOU. As a matter of fact, He authored your life and He leaves no chapter undone. The Bible tells us in Mark chapter 4 verses 21-22 that God is after your true self, the real you. That is who He sees. Stop hiding behind excuses, hardship, insecurities and REVEAL YOURSELF. Insignificance is a lie. Point to yourself and ask the question, "CAN YOU SEE ME?" The answer is a resounding YES, I SEE YOU!

You reflect an image that no one else can. Look around. If God made all things, then we cannot ignore that God is into variety and diversity. He didn't make us all the same. We are different in race, voice, shape, and gender. Don't tell me God is not into uniqueness. He made everything for a purpose. Everything about you has purpose.

> You reflect an image that no one else can.

There are things that you have to say that can only be said by you. Your voiceprint in the earth is vital to another human's success. There are things that when you touch them, they prosper. No two fingerprints are alike. Think about it. Why? Because there are things that only you can touch. Our meaning and significance come from Him and Him only.

Colossians 1:16 MSG

Everything got started in Him and finds its purpose in Him.

Outside of Him you have no purpose. Start with Him. Why were you created? Ask Him those questions audaciously. Or else life for you will never have true meaning.

Jeremiah caught onto this. He knew to ask a question.

Jeremiah 20:18 TEV

Why was I born? Was it only to have trouble and sorrow, to end life in disgrace?

I think Jeremiah was being a bit audacious and sarcastic. He was like look, Lord, is this what life is all about… trouble, sorrows? He went on to say, "Why didn't you just kill me in my mother's womb." Dang, Jeremiah, self-pity much? You wanted to be aborted? You will notice many Bible characters demonstrated suicidal tendencies. I have worked with people who have contemplated suicide. I have discovered many don't really want to die, they just want to end their lives. I help them with that. Living a life outside of purpose sucks. Let's end it and begin again, a life of purpose.

Here is a scripture I use when ministering to them:

Psalm 51:12 TPT

Let my passion for life be restored, tasting joy in every breakthrough you bring to me. Hold me close to you with a willing spirit that obeys whatever you say.

Jeremiah's story doesn't end there. In the very next chapter, we see him being a mouthpiece for God and overthrowing Kingdoms. I thank God for his audacity to continue beyond what he felt. At least he asked God and not man. God has a way of answering with results.

Jeremiah asked God why didn't He kill him in his mother's womb. If we realize that our purposes started before the womb, we would stop killing babies. He purposed our lives, planned it out even before we were conceived. If you ever get amnesia about why you are here, you need a reminder. Just ask God to reveal what He had in mind before you were a thought in mommy's and daddy's minds.

Psalm 139:13-16 NLT

You made all the delicate, inner parts of my body and knit me together in my mother's womb. Thank you for making me so wonderfully complex! Your workmanship is marvelous—how well I know it. You watched me as I was being formed in utter seclusion, as I was woven together in the dark of the womb. You saw me before I was born. Every day of my life was recorded in your book. Every moment was laid out before a single day had passed.

Don't allow anyone to make you feel insignificant. Not even your own thoughts. Thoughts like there is nothing special about you, or even thoughts that you don't produce like everyone else.

I remember feeling invisible. It was not a regular feeling for me, but it was one that came on a certain day every year, Mother's Day.

A day I dreaded for years in my journey of fertility. Let me tell you about the day I had the audacity to end that.

"I AM STANDING THIS YEAR!"

It was May of 2003—Mother's Day. I had just suffered a pregnancy loss and honestly, it took a lot to even get up to attend church that morning. I have such a deep conviction that nothing will separate me from God's love and my situation was trying to separate me that morning. I went anyway. It was Mother's Day. A constant reminder that I wasn't a mother.

Thing is, that reminder never came from me, it came from everyone else. The moment I hit the door, everybody was saying, "Happy Mother's Day"! but then they would catch glimpses of me and apologize. I thought, *No need to apologize, I will always say "Thank you, same to you."* As I approached the doors of the sanctuary, the greeters were handing out flowers. "Are you a mom? Here you go," they said to everyone in front of me.

I extended my hand out and here comes the showstopper, the moment that everyone will really know if I am saved for real. The words that could literally take me to a place that she wasn't ready for. "Sorry this is for the mothers," she said. I immediately saw myself rip that horrible wig off her head and snatch every rose she had in her hand, ripping them to shreds along with her matted tangled synthetic hair. I came to myself and said gently, "I would like one, thank you."

I got to my seat and soon it was time for all the mothers to stand. A special prayer was going to be said over the mothers. As I place my hand on the arm rest of the seat to assist me with standing, my neighbor sitting next to me touched me on my left shoulder and said in a very pitiful voice, "Don't worry, you will be standing next year." I'd had enough! I looked him square in the eye, raised my voice and said, "I AM STANDING THIS YEAR!" "Are you a Mother"? he asked. "YES, I AM!"

Mother's Day can bring about many emotions. Excitement because it's finally time for you to be celebrated for a job that can never receive enough thanks. It can also bring about sadness and pain because you've dreamed about being a mother and it just hasn't happened yet. Maybe you are battling infertility. Maybe it is a reminder of a child that died or even your own mother who has passed.

Let's be proactive by not allowing our emotions to lie to us. Instead of burying the memory and masking the pain, I encourage people to celebrate the time you had with your mother. Remember something funny about her and allow it to stir up a joy that releases such ability to overcome any sorrow.

If you lost a child and you went on to have three more, remind yourself that you have four children. Heaven is more real than this Earth and your baby is living and growing in heaven, having a ball. They are eternally connected to you. You will always be their mother. Trust me, there will be a reunion when you get there. And if you are still waiting for a baby to hold in your arms, don't tell yourself or let anyone else tell you that you are not a mother. YOU CERTAINLY ARE.

See you have to HAVE something before you have it. You have to SEE it before it manifests. Allow yourself to dream again because the time will come when that child will look at you and call you mother. Until then grab your rose, stand to your feet, and call yourself MOTHER! I sure did that day and four years later it was my reality.

You have to TAKE what belongs to you without asking. You have to reject the labels put on you by people. I refused to be known as the lady that can't have a baby. Don't label me infertile because that is not what God calls me. I lay hold to what He says about me and you should too. Don't answer to names that were never in your blueprint. Take a stand against labels.

Vision, Purpose and Intentionality

We have to live in purpose and on purpose. Life will always come to test the authenticity of your purpose. Don't be thrown off by the test. In those times you simply need clarity, and vision clarifies purpose. Don't be afraid of intentionality. Be intentional in life.

When you discover your life's purposes and write down the vision for your life, it simplifies things. But here is the thing, you can't write the vision one time. Don't live off of yesterday's manna. Visions evolve. God doesn't change, but He does leave things covered for appointed times. It may simply be time for a revealing of part of the vision you didn't know before. The Bible says in Deuteronomy 8:3 that *man does not live by bread alone but by every word that proceeds out of the mouth of God does a man live*. That sentence literally looks like it is moving. Which indicates that word is still proceeding out of His mouth. What is God saying today to you about your life? Find out and write it down. Write it down for every area of your life.

> Don't live off of yesterday's manna.

Vision can do a lot of things for you. Vision can cause discipline in your life because it can control your choices. It can dictate decisions you make daily because inside of your vision is destination. Vision will stop you from loading everything on your plate. When you have vision, you will realize you were not born to cover everything and that's ok. It's ok to be multi-faceted and multi-talented. It sets you up for destiny; just be careful of overwhelming yourself when you don't have to.

I've noticed that influential people are intentional. Let's take my boy Joshua; we will talk to him soon. His vision came from God as soon as he stepped on the scene to lead. But he had to meditate on the Word of God day and night to get clarity. Meditation brings clarity. Meditation causes you to see beyond today. During the ministry of Jesus, He was intentional. Think about the pool of Bethesda. He could have healed many people, but He healed one guy. There was intentionality in that.

Stress is produced from being all over the place. You are too important and significant to die from stress. Your purpose should produce boundaries. You can't do what everybody else can. You can't go where everyone else can. You can choose to, but you shouldn't. I've noticed those things you do that you should not do, you become a slave to them.

1 Corinthians 6:12 NLT

You say, "I am allowed to do anything"—but not everything is good for you. And even though "I am allowed to do anything," I must not become a slave to anything.

Don't be a jack-of-all-trades and a master of none. You become the best influential leader when you find the thing you are supposed to master. Your significance will even be realized with others. When people know who you are, they will come to you for who you are. Don't be so general. God is not general. He is detailed. Have you read the Bible lately?

A vision that was terminated by trials probably was not authentic. Think about Nelson Mandela's vision of ending apartheid. That vision took him to prison, but his vision was not terminated. Your dream may not seem massive, but it is significant. The mark it makes will never be erased.

Rosa Parks taking a seat on a bus one day seemed so insignificant at the time, but it made a mark that will never be erased. Mary pouring oil on the feet of Jesus at the time may have seemed insignificant. But it was for His burial. A mark that will never be erased. We still talk and preach about that woman today.

Your vision should solve a problem. Ask yourself, *What problems am I currently solving?* My vision solves the identity crisis problem. I know I am put here on this Earth for discovery. To help people find out who they really are. Have I been doing that as you read?

Your vision will choose your use of time, energy, what you read, your friends, your hobbies, etc. It can take you beyond what you have and create resources. Vision will make you take a risk in faith and see without limits. It inspires passion. Vision is the thought that won't leave you. Now that's significant. What do you ponder on daily? It's the recurring dream. You even see that dream while you are awake.

I love God so much. I know He hides vision inside of His people.

We just have to make time for discovery. We have to use our imagination. Put pictures to what we see. My husband spent months helping me to realize the importance of imagination. He helped me to realize that God created us to be image makers. I learned to see with the eyes of my heart. It moved me out of the constraints and limitations of the physical realm and put me into a spiritual reality and that realm is outside of this natural world. It will kill any thoughts or feelings of insignificance.

When those feelings come, take your mind off yourself and begin to magnify the Lord. When you do that you are bringing the reality of who He is to influence what is temporarily happening to you in that moment. To shrink any problem, you have to magnify the solution and He is always the solution.

Magnification ignites your imagination and presents you with a new reality. Remember the account of Paul and Silas in jail? I think about Silas in this situation. It was Paul who made those folk mad. Silas was just the sidekick, seemingly insignificant. Silas could have really complained, but they both began to magnify the Lord. It painted a different picture for them.

Think about it, when you are praising God (I hope you spend time praising God.), your imagination activates. You are not thinking about the problem, you are thanking God for the solution. Many times in the moment your eyes are closed, and you are seeing the solution as you are jumping, crying, waving, falling out or whatever you find yourself doing. Magnification is igniting your imagination and bringing you a new reality.

> I didn't give my entire life to a supernatural being to live naturally. That's boring.

Consider Peter, who walked on water. Where did he get that idea from? He got that image from Jesus and imagined himself doing it. He defied natural law through his imagination, and it became his reality. I dare you to go walk on water. Before you do it, see it. It's time we all defied this natural realm. I didn't give my entire life to a supernatural being to live naturally. That's boring.

And while we are talking about imagination, I have to warn you, you can use your imagination negatively. You can keep your eyes on the rearview mirror of your past. That picture will give you a distorted window of your future. You see through bitterness, anger and unforgiveness, that window will keep you on repeat. You will hear the chorus of a song written in a time of your life that kept you lame. Before you know it, you will look up and it has been 38 years and you're still laying by the pool in your bed.

I learned to take what's in my imagination and make it something I can physically see through vision boards. You should see my wall in my office right now. I have the body of Fantasia and the cash of Bill Gates (LOL) in pictures.

Where I am concerned, nothing is insignificant. I pay attention to everything. God is in the details. He is in conversations, nature, dreams, open vision, everything. Everything about you is significant to Him. Absolutely everything. He didn't just haphazardly make you. He formed every detail of you.

This scripture describes your significance to God so beautifully. Read it slowly.

Psalm 139: 1-18 TPT

You are so intimately aware of me, Lord. You read my heart like an open book and you know all the words I'm about to speak before I even start a sentence! You know every step I will take before my journey even begins.

Every single moment you are thinking of me! How precious and wonderful to consider that you cherish me constantly in your every thought! O God, your desires toward me are more than the grains of sand on every shore! When I awake each morning, you're still with me. Lord, you know everything there is to know about me. You perceive every movement of my heart and soul, and you understand my every thought before it even enters my mind.

You've gone into my future to prepare the way, and in kindness you follow behind me to spare me from the harm of my past. With your hand of love upon my life, you impart a blessing to me. This is just too wonderful, deep, and incomprehensible! Your understanding of me brings me wonder and strength. Where could I go from your Spirit? Where could I run and hide from your face? If I go up to heaven, you're there! If I go down to the realm of the dead, you're there too! If I fly with wings into the shining dawn, you're there! If I fly into the radiant sunset, you're there waiting! Wherever I go, your hand will guide me; your strength will empower me. It's impossible to disappear from you or to ask the darkness to hide me, for your presence is everywhere, bringing light into my night. There is no such thing as darkness with you. The night, to you, is as bright as the day; there's no difference between the two. You formed my innermost being, shaping my delicate inside and my intricate outside, and wove them all together in my mother's womb. I thank you, God, for making me so mysteriously complex! Everything you do is marvelously breathtaking. It simply amazes me to think about it! How thoroughly you know me, Lord! You even formed every bone in my body when you created me in the secret place, carefully, skillfully shaping me from nothing to something. You saw who you created me to be before I became me! Before I'd ever seen the light of day, the number of days you planned for me were already recorded in your book.

Now go back and read it again. There is something you didn't get the first time you read it.

Let's do the work:

When it comes to your vision, in what areas do you need to pray for clarity or evolution?

Sum up your vision in a mission statement. No more than three sentences.

What is your recurring dream?

What is a thought that you ponder on daily?

What problem does your vision solve?

What does Psalm 139:1-18 mean to you?

CHAPTER FOUR

Mind Your Business

Drag your thoughts away from your troubles...by the ears, by the heels or any other way you can manage it. -Mark Twain

There is no way I can write a book titled Audacity, be your midwife and not deal with your mind, your thinking and your mindsets. Your greatest enemy is not the devil. Your greatest enemy is you. Your limits come from your thinking. From wrong mindsets that may have been established since childhood.

This chapter may be a rollercoaster for you but take the ride. Those ups and downs should lead to a final destination of mental stability. I am humbled by the assignments I get from heaven. It was last year in 2018 when God led me to begin unpacking our mental health. My objective is to shed light on some very dark areas, to loose the chains of bondages that are on people concerning mental health and to simply open a conversation about it. I will provide antidotes and answers to overcome any stronghold that you are dealing with from trauma or sin—generational or situational.

Disclaimer: I am not a doctor or a mental health professional.

I am a pastor. I will approach this from a biblical viewpoint, understanding that science is wrapped up in it. You really can't separate science and God. I believe science is the details of God. I also believe your answers for your mental health can be found in the Word of God.

It is my prayer that the church and the mental health community will form partnerships in this time to minister to the whole man, touching the psychological, spiritual and emotional areas of people's lives. I don't think we have to put one down to elevate another. It can all exist together. God placed us all on Earth for a purpose and we have to respect and honor each other's purposes and vocations in life to serve humanity.

Together we have to be like Jesus and say, "For this reason have I manifested, to destroy the works of the enemy." Our partnerships can help people walk in wholeness and live healthy from the inside out.

It has been my desire to help in this area since I was a teenager. I have been preaching the gospel since I was a teen. I remember being asked to speak at a youth retreat that was being held up in the mountains of Pennsylvania. This was my first time really speaking outside of my normal youth group, and I was excited and really felt ready. It was my night to minister and I felt the power of God. I knew God was going to do something amazing that night.

I was excited. I spoke to the young people about letting go of things that were holding them back from serving God. I talked about the three Hebrew boys and their stand to not bow to any golden images. I told them they can live for God at a young age, that they shouldn't wait until they are older to enjoy a life with God. God ignited that place. We found ourselves in deep worship when I was led to make an altar call. I felt that there were some young people there who were bound by some demonic activity, trauma and bitterness towards their parents; I knew as a result it had caused some mental health issues.

So me being the bold young woman I was, I called it out and told them to come to the altar so I could pray with them. I was going to lay my hands on them. So I moved forward in boldness for the first time. I called out the devil that had been holding these young people back. I began to invite them to the altar. They came, 13, 14, 15 and 16 year olds, crying, screaming, wanting to be free. Other youth leaders joined me at the altar to receive these young people.

The altar was full. I wanted to minister to them one by one. I noticed a girl who looked like she was really pressing in for something, I felt led to pray for her first. I grabbed her hands and immediately felt led to ask her what she came for. My eyes were drawn to her arms where it was clear she was a "cutter." As I looked back into her eyes she began to tell me something that would grab for my compassion.

She told me that she really wanted to forgive her father for killing her mother. The murder happened in front of her. She went on to say, "I replay it in my mind and because I didn't do anything to help her, I cut." At that moment I laid hands on her differently than you would imagine. I embraced her, and in that moment, I became her mother. I rocked her as she cried and screamed. I told her as her mother, I forgave her, and it wasn't her fault.

I honestly believe Holy Spirit healed her in that moment. We stayed there a long time. For us, time stood still. But once that time was over, I left and all I could think about was her. Today, self-injury exists with 1 in 5 females and 1 in 7 males. They are among us but masked. My heart still aches for them.

I knew enough at that time that she needed therapy. That she needed tools to maintain her freedom and get to "free indeed." I knew these same emotions would try to return because of triggers she may have from the trauma. I now know how to properly apply the cross to these situations, but I didn't know then. I left her feeling incomplete and inadequate. While she left me feeling free, I prayed for her free indeed.

I now know your thought patterns are so key to true freedom. When we realize how this controls our lives, we will truly think about what we think about. We will have a new revelation of this scripture:

2 Corinthians 10:4-5

(For the weapons of our warfare are not carnal, but mighty through God to the pulling down of strong holds;) Casting down imaginations, and every high thing that exalteth itself against the knowledge of God, and bringing into captivity every thought to the obedience of Christ;

This scripture is cognitive, meaning it deals with the mind primarily. Here we realize that we have a battlefield called the mind. The good news is that we have weapons for this battle. The weapons we have demolish strongholds. Strongholds exist in our minds. Our thoughts can truly keep us bound and produce a stronghold that will control, lie and manipulate you.

When you think about the word stronghold, that the Bible uses to refer to your mind, I want you to think about the words block, barricade, buffer, wall, security and deterrence.

These strongholds are darkness the enemy uses to *block out the truth.* You will build a wall of defense in your mind to protect the lies and keep the truth out. Like the lie when you are in a meaningful relationship but because of your past experience you believe that if you don't sleep with them, they will leave you or cheat on you. Or the lie that the spirit of poverty inserts that says you cannot give or tithe because you will always be broke, so keep everything you get to take care of yourself. You can't really trust God.

The enemy will take real life issues, historical things that have happened and make them so real in the present. For example, you have been in a horrible car accident, so you don't drive. Or you flinch every time someone gets close to your car. It distorts what is going on and perpetuates cycles in your life. That is evidence of a stronghold's existence in your life.

Mental strongholds are like tainted glasses you look through and don't know you are wearing them. Like someone placed them on you while you were sleep. You cannot cast out strongholds; you can only pull them down. There are areas in our minds where darkness reigns and as a result, spiritual perception grows dim.

I have seen these strongholds in people's lives twist scriptures to conform to their own self-serving premises. They erect doctrine in their lives based on bad experiences that go against the truth of God's word. For instance, they believed God for a loved one to be healed of cancer and they still died. Somehow to protect the lie because of what they may have called failure, they believe that God is not a healer. Their patterns place command posts in our lives through which the enemy can gain access. For me it's where the spirit of fear was able to take up residence and use my imagination to create misperceptions.

While working as a government contractor, I traveled a lot. I never had an issue with flying before the day I let the spirit of fear gain access. I was on a flight headed to the west coast with a co-worker. I typically don't really pay attention to the stewardess during the safety protocols they give before take-off. So while I was browsing through the choice of in-flight movies, my co-worker nudged me pretty hard and just as I was about to return that gesture with a push that would have knocked her out of her seat, I looked in her eyes and saw this authoritative-type seriousness that I had never seen before.

"What!" I exclaimed loudly and irritably. She responded, "Pay attention," like I was a 5 year old distracted by my toys while my parents were talking to me.

"Why?" I asked her.

"Because you are on this plane with me and this is how I know I am going to die." My thoughts went wild, "Come again, say what?" I'd boarded this plane with an absolute lunatic, and I have 5 hours of this. "Ummm, how do you know this is the way you are going to die?"

Now asking this question should have led me to minister to her, but instead the enemy was about to gain access to my soul and the spirit of fear was about to move in with all sorts of bags and furniture. I listened to her talk about how many bad experiences she'd had on planes and how she had already lost someone to a plane crash. Right there I should have stopped her and realized when that person died, she too stopped living.

She talked about her bad luck and how we all have to go sometime, and this was the way she was going to go. She kept saying, "… and you are going to be traveling with me, so I should warn you." Now, I know you are reading this and picturing her saying this sarcastically and us having a light joking moment, but it wasn't that at all. The Spirit of fear was bouncing around while she was talking looking for an entry point.

What I should have done was tell her to shut up and then cast down the thoughts that were entering my mind, but I kept listening, thinking, *This girl is crazy, and I don't need to travel with her anymore.* I began to magnify her words and think, *This chick is going to take us down*, and I kid you not, right there in the middle of that thought there was turbulence like I have never experienced.

I wondered if I was sitting with the devil himself. The pilot got on the intercom and asked us to buckle up because the next few moments would be rough. She looked at me and said, "I told you." I started sweating with my born-again, talking-in-tongues, casting-out-demons self. I began to look out of the window and wonder, *How do airplanes actually fly*? and *How do we know if our plane has mechanical issues? You don't know until you dead. Flying is stupid. It's such a risk.*

All these thoughts flooded my mind, and my heart pounded that entire flight and several flights after. I had developed a fear of flying. A fear that came through a conversation. An outcome that someone had resolved that was made up.

Most of our fears are made up. We magnify them and make them real and bring them into our reality. For at least two years, I had to take medicine to get on flights and keep me calm. I had stewards to walk me up and down the aisles during flights to keep me calm. Rubbing my back and giving me water, just ridiculous. Sounds ridiculous now, but that bondage had me tripping. Much like your fear of spiders and heights and not allowing your children to leave the house—all strongholds! Thank God what God reveals He heals.

My deliverance was in two parts. I went to church and my pastor was preaching a series on the spirit of fear. I ate that word every Sunday, like it was meat and potatoes. I didn't miss a service. I would go home and go over the scriptures while listening to the tape (it was long ago). I played those tapes until they broke.

When he ended the series, he had an altar call to cast out that spirit of fear. I think I was the first one to the altar. I knew if I lingered that spirit would lie to me and tell me that I was ok. I was the first one there, hands up, ready to be free. When my pastor laid his hand on me, I knew it left me. I knew it. I felt it, I grabbed freedom.

But here was the second step. I know what the scripture says about being delivered of a stronghold or when you have allowed a strongman to take up residence in your life and you get free of it. It is clear about how an unclean spirit returns.

Luke 11:24-26 NKJV

*24 When an unclean spirit goes out of a man, he goes through dry
places, seeking rest; and finding none, he says, 'I will return to my
house from which I came.' 25 And when he comes, he finds it swept
and put in order. 26 Then he goes and takes with him seven other*

spirits more wicked than himself, and they enter and dwell there; and the last state of that man is worse than the first.

John 14:30 AMPC

*30 I will not talk with you much more, for the prince (evil genius, ruler) of the world is coming. And he has no claim on Me. [**He has nothing in common with Me; there is nothing in Me that belongs to him, and he has no power over Me.**] [emphasis added]*

When you get delivered of an unclean spirit you cannot leave your house empty. You have to fill those places in you so that when the unclean spirit tries to return, and it will, it will see that your house is occupied! You are not that empty person anymore. Ephesians 4:27 Amplified Bible (AMP) says, "Leave no such room or foothold for the devil [give no opportunity to him]."

There is no ROOM in my mind, no room in my will, how I make my decisions, and certainly devil, there is NO ROOM in the area of my emotions for you to come and take up residence. **It's occupied; I will not leave you any room and you have no power over me!**

That's that. That spirit of fear is a spirit, and it needed to be cast out, and I had to make sure it didn't return. Now, there was a different process with the mental stronghold. I could no longer take on the thoughts that the spirit of fear tried to intrude with. I had to cast them down. I had to renew my mind where fear was concerned. This is a continual process.

The Bible refers to Jesus as the stronger man. He really is. Nothing can match the strength of God. Nothing can stand up against Him.

He has no rival. The world of darkness is not His equal. Your life's confession needs to be that HE is your stronghold.

Psalm 18:2 ESV

The LORD is my rock and my fortress and my deliverer,
my God, my rock, in whom I take refuge,
my shield, and the horn of my salvation, ***my stronghold****.*
[emphasis added]

PSALM 27:1 ESV

The LORD is my light and my salvation;
whom shall I fear?
The LORD is the ***stronghold*** *of my life;*
of whom shall I be afraid? [emphasis added]

The Bible talks about serving two masters. While that scripture is dealing with money, the principle applies in every area of your life. You really can't serve two masters. Eventually you will head one way or the other. Anything that does not align itself with God's will for you is a place of darkness and it defines something you have in common with darkness. Don't associate with darkness. Do what the scripture says, take those thoughts captive.

To take captive means to capture. It means to force into submission. Have the audacity to take captive those thoughts that go against the word of God. I once asked the question, "How do I make my mind, mind?"

Here are a few answers to that question:

1. You don't have to believe everything you think. Negative

emotions can cause us to lie to ourselves. Truth is truth. Truth doesn't change. Truth is not a river that flows and changes with the tide or the culture. Truth is a ROCK. Many of us have lived out lies long enough. Unfortunately, we have built our lives on lies or as the Bible says, sand. You cannot build on sand.

2. Stop playing in trash. Trash produces stinking thinking. Proverbs 15:14 (NLT) says, "A wise person hungers for the truth while the fool feeds on trash." Stop being a fool. You have to watch filling your mind with junk food. It spoils your appetite for the right nutrition you need to grow. Psalm 101:3 (ESV) says, "I will not set before my eyes anything that is worthless."

   Focus on things that are good instead of focusing on bad things. Many times, we have bad thoughts and we do our best to cast them off. But I want to give you a new strategy. Don't focus so much on casting them off as much as I want you to focus on replacing the thought. Once you cast it down, replace it with truth. I like to say, simply turn the channel and input something else.

   I once heard a man of God say that we have to treat our thoughts like trains. Grand Central Station in New York has trains that pull in and out of the station all day, every day. Just like you will have trains of thoughts all day every day, 24 hours a day. When you get on the wrong "train," simply get off and get on a new train. Don't be surprised when you hear me saying, "Portia,-get off that train." It is something I practice regularly.

3. Learn something new every day. It is so key to staying away from old thoughts. Always remain a student and constantly learn. Proverbs 18:15 (NLT) says, "Intelligent people are always ready to learn. Their ears are open to knowledge."

4. Renew your mind daily with God's word. It's loaded with power to renew. I believe Romans chapter 12 verse 2 is the cure for any memory loss. We have to renew our minds. It is a daily process. We should never stop renewing our minds.

5. Use your imagination. Allow yourself to dream constantly. Dream while you are awake. Be intentional and spend time daily doing this. During the summer and spring months I take time and go on imagination walks. I just walk with God and imagine with him. Doing that gave me a new outlook on Ephesians 3:20, "Now unto him that is able to do exceeding abundantly above all that we ask or think, according to the power that worketh in us."

Practice these steps daily. You are mentally stronger than you know. You absolutely don't have to allow your mind to run wild or even run you. Every thought you think is not even your thought. You do not have to ponder. You can replace it. All day long we are always thinking and choosing. It's a nonstop action that happens passively every day. I want you for the next week to think about what you are thinking about. Why am I asking you to do that?

Proverbs 4:23 New Century Version (NCV)

Be careful what you think, because your thoughts run your life.

Your thoughts run your life! Knowing that, don't leave your

thought life up for grabs. Be intentional and audacious about guarding it.

Romans 12:2 TPT

Stop imitating the ideals and opinions of the culture around you, but be inwardly transformed by the Holy Spirit through a total ***reformation of how you think.*** *This will empower you to discern God's will as you live a beautiful life, satisfying and perfect in his eyes.[emphasis added]*

OMgeeeee did you see that? You can **reform** how you think. Christian Scientist, Dr. Caroline Leaf has studied the brain intently. She has discovered that thoughts are *designed* to be redesigned.

She communicates that it takes 21 days to receive a new thought and three cycles of that to form a new habit, that is 63 days. You can do this! If you are stuck in your thought life, have the audacity to start today. The scripture says it will lead to a beautiful life.

I believe in the healing power of God. I also believe in the same way you can be sick in your body, you can also be sick in your mind. Jesus died for that as well. Some things are actually not illness; they are simply sin and trauma that we have not applied the grace of God to.

It doesn't have to be taboo to talk about it. We have to face it head on. We cannot be afraid of the doctors, the diagnosis, the stigmas or the unsaid. I tell people all the time, when you are in a bad place (and you know when you are in a bad place), never consult yourself. Don't go into isolation. You need to get help.

We see the prophet Elijah make this mistake in 1 Kings.

1 Kings 19:1-3 NKJV

And Ahab told Jezebel all that Elijah had done, also how he had executed all the prophets with the sword. [2] Then Jezebel sent a messenger to Elijah, saying, "So let the gods do to me, and more also, if I do not make your life as the life of one of them by tomorrow about this time." [3] And when he saw that, he arose and ran for his life, and went to Beersheba, which belongs to Judah, and left his servant there

Jezebel issued a threat by way of Ahab to Elijah. She basically said, "I am going to kill you." He goes on the run and doesn't take his assistant. That was a bad idea. First of all, don't run from empty threats. Second, always take someone on your journey of pain.

God wants to deal with the whole man: spirit, soul and body. He died for all of you. Just like He is Father, Son and Holy Ghost, the trinity, three in one, you too are a three-part being. You are spirit, soul and body. This area of your soul is so important to living a prosperous life. The Bible says in 1 John 3:2, "Beloved, I wish above all things that thou mayest prosper and be in health, even as thy soul prospereth."

Knowing how you were created is important to your health. If you are not healthy in your soul, then you won't see health in your body. Your spirit is the highest part of you. Your spirit is you in communion with God, your worship, but it is also your conscience and your intuition. It is where Holy Spirit lives. Your soul consists of your mind, your will and your emotions. I also like to say your feeler, your chooser and your thinker.

Last of all your body is the physical substance we see every day.

What you need to understand is that your mind is in your soul, and your mind affects your brain. Your brain obviously is in your body and that is what the medical community can see, your brain, but not your soul. Many sicknesses, both physical and mental, are in your soul and they come out in your body.

Can I tell you that God is brilliant? His design of us is brilliant. He designed you so that through your mind, which is in your soul, you can change your brain. When you have toxic thoughts, they cause inflammation in the brain. Your brain is designed to follow your mind. With that in mind (no pun intended), we cannot allow our thoughts to run rampant.

Overcoming Depression

Depression is a state of hopelessness. It is currently the leading cause of illness in our generation. It is easy to self-medicate through drinking, drugs, sex and overeating or whatever else you use so you won't feel. That is temporary and certainly not the answer.

Depression is defined as a mood disorder that results in an inability to experience pleasure. It is a syndrome that deprives people of energy, sleep, concentration, joy, confidence, memory and sex drive. It robs people of their ability to love, work and play. It can take your will to live, and if not dealt with over time, it can damage the brain and wreak havoc on the body. Depression comes as a result of stress and pressures that have been internalized. This is why it is vital to have some sort of community in your life. You need to have healthy conversations about your feelings and emotions. We are not robots. Depression can also be a result of external pressure that weighs you down. The Bible tells us to cast all of our cares on Him. All of them.

1 Peter 5:7 AMP

7 casting all your cares [all your anxieties, all your worries, and all your concerns, once and for all] on Him, for He cares about you [with deepest affection, and watches over you very carefully].

1 Peter 5:7 TPT

Pour out all your worries and stress upon him and leave them there, for he always tenderly cares for you.

Other symptoms of depression are reclusiveness. A person with these symptoms thinks it's ok to spend life by themselves. God did not create man to be alone. One of the first things He did in the garden was give man a companion. People who are anti-social and have hermit tendencies are reclusive. They are more interested in technology than people. These people withdraw from reality. They have issues with concentration.

People experiencing depression are often passive. They have an "I don't care" attitude. They also have a tendency to magnify issues, like making mountains out of molehills.

God knows the destruction that can occur when our cares are not cast on Him. Anxieties, worries and concerns not cast off can form into depression. He did not design us to carry cares. The words "I don't care" are the most powerful words in the English language, but you have to mean it. We say I don't care, and not only do we care, we are hurting emotionally and physically from the care.

I learned through the PAIRS foundation, established for military couples that cope with deployment and being away from their families, how to really cast my cares. You may be asking, Is Portia military? Nope, I am just hungry for answers and who better to help with that than people who deal with emotional trauma all the time.

The activity is called "Emptying the Emotional Jug." Emotions were not meant to be bottled up. Holding things inside can cause imploding. You will burst inwardly. The thing about imploding is it grows stronger while being held inside. You will eventually begin to "leak" and that is not a pretty process. When you leak because of imploding, it comes out through sarcasm, ridiculing, threatening, labeling, taunting, lying or withholding and the like. But it also may not display as active. It may be more passive, like ignoring people, blaming, hiding (physically) or not being actively present.

How do you empty this? You have to get with someone, and the following questions have to be asked with honest answers provided. If you are not going to be honest, then you are not going to be free.

- What are you sad about?
- What are you mad about?
- What are you confused about?
- What has caused you to be disappointed?

Answer these questions until you are empty of all those negative emotions. Be patient and get through the process.

Why is depression so prevalent in our generation?

Depression is primarily lifestyle related. Here is great news, if it can be created by your lifestyle, it can be changed by your lifestyle. If you study civilization—Western vs. Eastern, different cultures and generations, and follow the statistics—it is amazing what you will discover. Only one known group of Americans hasn't been hit by the modern depression epidemic: the Amish.

They are still clinging audaciously to their eighteenth-century way of life. Amish communities have a rate of depression dramatically lower than that of the general population. In Eastern civilization the mental illness statistics are very low, but once they try to become like Americans, it goes up.

I am going to tell you like I want to tell the Eastern civilizations, don't do it. Don't bankrupt yourself trying to be like someone else. Don't look at yourself and look at someone else and say, I am not enough. Comparison is a killer. Know yourself; you are too unique to be compared fairly.

When I was seeking God for answers regarding the state of our mental health, He said one word to me that made so much sense. Idolatry. Idolatry is anyone or anything that replaces the one true God. We seek things outside of God to fulfill and then make them gods in our lives. It is worship of an idol or image. It is looking to other things to provide ultimate fulfillment in our lives.

You may think, well that's too far, that ain't me. No, we are not melting down our gold jewelry, giving it a name and dancing around it. But think about the things you put before God. It's packaged differently. What about the people you put before Him? Ask yourself where do you go to get satisfaction? Ask yourself what *good* things have you promoted to *God* things. In my life personally the way I have crushed idolatry is through craving God. I had to starve everything else and make Him my only option. Options are the enemy to hunger. Eliminate all other options.

Psalm 16:2 Modern English Version (MEV)

I have said to the Lord, "You are my Lord; my welfare has no existence outside of You."

God is our greatest good and knowing Him is the highest satisfaction man can ever have.

The Bible is actually pretty comical at times. The one thing in life I don't want to be is a fool. That word just bothers me, and the Bible defines a fool many times and in many ways. In Proverbs 18:2 it says that the fool lacks understanding and is always expressing their opinion.

In Proverbs 1:17 it says fools despise instruction, and one of my all-time favorites in Proverbs 18:6 pretty much says a fool's mouth deserves blows, so when I hit you in your mouth just know I am in the Bible. Ok, I am just kidding, I think. Romans talks about a fool as it relates to idolatry.

Romans 1:21-23 TPT

Throughout human history the fingerprints of God were upon them, yet they refused to honor him as God or even be thankful for his kindness. Instead, they entertained corrupt and foolish thoughts about what God was like. This left them with nothing but misguided hearts, steeped in moral darkness. Although claiming to be wise, they were in fact shallow fools. For only a fool would trade the unfading splendor of the immortal God to worship the fading image of other humans, idols made to look like people, animals, birds, and even creeping reptiles!"

Well that's pretty clear. Only a fool would trade worshipping God for worshipping other humans, animals or things.

Judges 10:11-14 God's Word Translation (GW)

The LORD said to the people of Israel, "When the Egyptians, the Amorites, the Ammonites, the Philistines, the Sidonians, the Amalekites, and the Maonites oppressed you, you cried out to me for help. Didn't I rescue you from them? But you still abandoned me and served other gods. That's why I won't rescue you again. Cry out for help to the gods you chose. Let them rescue you when you're in trouble."

Basically, He was saying those idols can't help you. I get you out of trouble time and time again and you keep going back and worshipping and bowing down to the creation instead of the Creator. C'mon, let's not be those people.

Let's look at God's attitude in this scripture.

Hebrews 13:5 AMPC

5 Let your [a]character or moral disposition be free from love of money [including greed, avarice, lust, and craving for earthly possessions] and be satisfied with your present [circumstances and with what you have]; for He [God] [b]Himself has said, I will not in any way fail you nor [c]give you up nor leave you without support. [I will] not, [d][I will] not, [I will] not in any degree leave you helpless nor forsake nor [e]let [you] down ([f]relax My hold on you)! [[g]Assuredly not!]

Be satisfied with your present circumstances and what you have. MY GOD! That will preach. That sounds like when the Bible says Godliness with contentment is great gain. God says He will in no way fail you or relax His hold on you. Feel His hold on you today. Let it heal that depression you may be experiencing.

Listen, when God calls something foolishness we better listen up. In this next scripture you actually see foolishness leading to depression. Yup, I think He covered it all in this one.

Ecclesiastes 4: 4-7 The Living Bible (TLB)

[4] Then I observed that the basic motive for success is the driving force of envy and jealousy! But this, too, is foolishness, chasing the wind. [5-6] The fool won't work and almost starves but feels that it is better to be lazy and barely get by, than to work hard, when in the long run it is all so futile.

[7] I also observed another piece of foolishness around the earth. [8] This is the case of a man who is quite alone, without a son or brother, yet he works hard to keep gaining more riches. And to whom will he leave it all, and why is he giving up so much now? It is all so pointless and depressing.

Dealing with Stress

Let me be honest with you, stress is largely unavoidable. You will deal with some type of stressors each day. Think about it, you go to work and have to sit in traffic-stress, you have a disagreement in your marriage-stress, you get an unexpected bill-stress, your child brings home a bad report-stress. This can go on all day. God knew this and made provisions for it in our creation.

Our brains have a clever stress response system that springs into action when stress shows up. According to scientists and medical research, it is short term. It is not designed to respond to long-term stress. That is not even supposed to be a thing. Here is what happens medically.

When we're stressed, our bodies release potent hormones like adrenaline and cortisol, which set in motion a host of other reactions. The liver dumps its stores of sugar into the bloodstream, providing booster fuel for the muscles. The lungs ramp up their intake of oxygen (another muscle fuel).

The heart beats faster and stronger, sending more nutrient-rich blood throughout the body. And the immune system shifts into tissue-repair mode to get ready for any injuries that might happen during a fight-or-flight encounter. Now just think about all that. That cannot happen all day, every day. This is why we have to cast our cares.

There may be seasons or times in our lives where we are extremely busy, but we should not live all of our lives like that. It may be doable, but it is not sustainable. It is an unjust balance.

Here are some things to consider when you are dealing with prolonged stress.

1. Stay refreshed spiritually and physically. Don't go over your budget. When you add something to your plate, ask yourself what did you take away. The Bible says in Ecclesiastes 4:6 NIV, "Better one handful with tranquility than two handfuls with toil." You have to know what you can handle. Every man has been given grace for their own lives. Know what your grace is.

2. Have regular meeting times and places with God. Make an altar in your car, on your walks, on the treadmill, in your bathroom. Whatever it takes, keep an environment where you experience the power and presence of God. I once heard someone say God doesn't have a speaking problem, we have a hearing problem. Turn down the noise of the world. Unplug from all media outlets.

3. Always stick with what God told you to do. Don't be bullied by the world and its expectations.

Anxiety

Anxiety comes from thoughts that repeat themselves over and over again. It comes from being extremely concerned. It's ok to be concerned about something, but concerns without a plan turn into worry. Worry can be viewed as concern on steroids. It will start to control you emotionally. That emotion is anxiety, and anxiety produces fear of something you think there is no way out of.

I have seen anxiety manifest many different ways. It can control your ability to sleep. You begin to lack the tools to cope. It can dictate how you start and run your day. When it manifests physically it looks like the following:

- Sweating
- Racing heart
- Uncontrollable tears
- Feeling of weakness
- Faintness

- Dizziness
- Tingling or numbness in hands
- Sense of unreality
- Sense of losing control or losing your mind
- Fear of dying or something physically wrong

Anxiety can produce some of the following nasty habits that become uncontrolled:

- Breaking the skin through intense scratching
- Rubbing out your hair
- Abuse of substances
- Hoarding
- Self-harm
- Eating disorders

Drive it Out: How to Be Free From Anxiety

I say drive it out because I believe it is a spirit. In 1 Samuel chapter 16 we find King Saul dealing with a tormenting spirit. The Bible says that tormenting spirit caused depression and fear, and he could not rest. David was called to play his harp and drive that spirit out of Saul.

Music sets atmospheres and creates environments. If you are dealing with anxiety, keep your atmosphere saturated with Godly music. In the referenced scripture, it wasn't necessarily in the lyrics, but the sound produced an atmosphere around him that drove out the evil spirit. You may want to keep a good playlist for playing at night; I do.

It also helps when your children are dealing with nightmares. Change the atmosphere in that room at night. Turn that television off, you have no clue what pops up at 2:00 a.m. and 3:00 a.m. Put on soaking music and set an atmosphere for the presence of God in your home.

Peace is anxiety's cure. Peace is more than just tranquility; it is the power of God to maintain a victory stance. Peace is audacious, it's militant and no spirit of anxiety can prevail against it. If you deal with anxiety, you cannot afford not to put the full armor of God on daily. Your feet have to be shod with the preparation of the gospel of peace. When we stand in peace the enemy cannot touch us.

Romans 16:20

20 *And the God of peace shall bruise Satan under your feet shortly. The grace of our Lord Jesus Christ be with you. Amen.*

He is the *God of peace*. That scripture makes me want to go into warfare for you, knowing Jesus is our peace and He will bruise Satan and put him under our feet. How dare he come against us like this and cause such torment.

John 14:27

27 *Peace I leave with you, my peace I give unto you: not as the world giveth, give I unto you. Let not your heart be troubled, neither let it be afraid.*

Make this confession daily: I will not be afraid because I live in continual peace! While making that confession allow peace to take over. You can live a life run by peace. Peace can call the shots and tell anxiety to "kick rocks."

Colossians 3:15 AMP

[15] Let the peace of Christ [the inner calm of one who walks daily with Him] be the controlling factor in your hearts [deciding and settling questions that arise]. To this peace indeed you were called as members in one body [of believers]. And be thankful [to God always].

When I personally was dealing with anxiety, I meditated on that scripture daily for an entire year. Peace became the controlling factor in my life. When questions came up that I could not answer that would typically cause anxiety, I allowed peace to answer. Peace was my clapback to anxiety! Don't just let anxiety take over and have rule. Allow peace to call the shots. Peace is the umpire of our lives.

Philippians 4:6-7 AMP

[6] Do not be anxious or worried about anything, but in everything [every circumstance and situation] by prayer and petition with thanksgiving, continue to make your [specific] requests known to God. [7] And the peace of God [that peace which reassures the heart, that peace] which transcends all understanding, [that peace which] stands guard over your hearts and your minds in Christ Jesus [is yours].

Another antidote is prayer and petition with thanksgiving. Keep a praise on your lips. It assists with magnifying the solution to anxiety. Evil spirits don't like hanging out where there is authentic praise and worship. I am not talking about singing about the problem like slaves but thanking Him for what is already done. Bowing in worship to Him so that you don't kneel to the emotions of anxiety.

Jesus was touched with EVERY FEELING of our infirmity. That means that He dealt with mental health. He dealt with it in the worst ways. All of them, every disease in the head, He experienced it.

Hebrews 4:15-16 NIV

For we do not have a high priest who is unable to empathize with our weaknesses, but we have one who has been tempted in every way, just as we are—yet he did not sin. Let us then approach God's throne of grace with confidence, so that we may receive mercy and find grace to help us in our time of need.

Jesus literally carried the weight of the world on His shoulders. He experienced anxiety and stress. Remember His time in the garden of Gethsemane?

Gethsemane was a meeting place for Jesus to pray. We hear mostly about it the night before Jesus' crucifixion, but it was a place where He met with God. I mentioned earlier when you are dealing with mental distresses you certainly need a regular meeting place with God. You have to unplug.

Mark 14:32-35 AMP

Then they went to a place called Gethsemane; and Jesus said to His disciples, "Sit down here until I have prayed." He took

Peter and James and John with Him, and He began to be ***deeply distressed and troubled [extremely anguishe****d at the prospect of what was to come]. And He said to them,* ***"My soul is deeply grieved and overwhelmed with sorrow, to the point of death [emphasis added]****; remain here and keep watch." After going a little farther, He fell to the ground [distressed by the weight of His spiritual burden] and began to pray that if it were possible [in the Father's will], the hour [of suffering and death for the sins of mankind] might pass from Him.*

All four gospels have slight variations, but in Luke's account an angel was sent to strengthen Him.

Let's look at the language Matthew used. It gives us a peek into the emotions Jesus experienced.

Matthew 26:36-39

Then Jesus came with them to a place called Gethsemane, and he told the disciples, "Sit here while I go over there and pray." Taking along Peter and the two sons of Zebedee, he began to be sorrowful (very strong Greek word that means horrified) and troubled. He said to them, "I am deeply grieved to the point of death. Remain here and stay awake with me." Going a little farther, he fell facedown and prayed, "My Father, if it is possible, let this cup pass from me. Yet not as I will, but as you will."

There are a few things I would like to highlight in both of these accounts so that you can get a full picture of what was happening. In Mark it says He was deeply distressed, and He took Peter, James and John with Him. Here we see Jesus being vulnerable in His mental struggle. I told you earlier don't walk through your pain of mental struggle alone. He said his soul was deeply grieved to the point of death. That sounds like suicidal thoughts.

Remember your soul is made up of your mind, will and emotions. I can imagine Jesus just wanting to end it right there. He could have, but He pressed past His emotions. It says He went a little further and fell to the ground. Jesus was through emotionally.

I began to research these passages a little deeper. In Matthew, the words "he began" denotes He began to see something He had never seen before. I believe Jesus got a glimpse of what was to come, and the scripture says He was sorrowful. Sorrowful is a really nice word used in the English language. But in the Greek language they use a different word that better describes the emotion. In the Greek it says He was horrified. The use of the words in Matthew paint a picture that He almost died under the strain of the stress of what was ahead.

Luke's account recorded blood. His emotions produced a physical reaction from His body. After putting that together I asked myself a few questions.

Why? Why the strain? What did He see? What was it? For the first time God was silent. He called out, "ABBA," a term of closest intimacy and received no response from His Father. His feelings of loneliness only increased when He went to the disciples whom He asked in His most vulnerable state to watch and pray, and they were asleep. Judgement had already begun. Right in those moments He was paying the ultimate price.

He saw you dealing with rejection and knew He had to take it on and overcome it. He saw you dealing with loneliness. The absence of His Father produced indiscernible emotions that He took on. He became depressed. The anxiety He experienced, it produced drops of blood. Our Jesus paid the ultimate price so that these things don't have to dominate us. He took on every form of mental illness in that garden.

Jesus knows how it feels to have a father say you are not my child. In one moment, He got a glimpse of all of hell and the emotions it puts on mankind. He saw what He would have to endure and was at every point touched and tempted, complete abandonment.

Gethsemane means oil press and that is exactly what was happening; the reality of God's wrath against our sins was pressing in on Him, literally squeezing the life out of Him. God showed Him in the garden because it was so important for Jesus to go to the cross voluntarily so that His love for us could be displayed even more. The greatest price of redemption.

This revelation brings tears to my eyes. I still ask Him why? "Why, Jesus, did you have to go through all this"? His answer: "Portia, for you. You were the Joy set before me that Hebrews 2:2 talks about. You are my Joy, and if I had to do it all over again I would." He told me anytime I am challenged mentally or overwhelmed with my emotions, cast it on Him.

With that revelation , let's look at 1 Peter a little closer.

1 Peter 5:6-11 AMP

Therefore humble yourselves under the mighty hand of God [set aside self-righteous pride], so that He may exalt you [to a place of honor in His service] at the appropriate time, casting all your cares [all your anxieties, all your worries, and all your concerns, once and for all] on Him, for He cares about you [with deepest affection, and watches over you very carefully]. Be sober [well balanced and self-disciplined], be alert and cautious at all times. That enemy of yours, the devil, prowls around like a roaring lion [fiercely hungry], seeking someone to devour. But resist him, be firm in your faith [against his attack--rooted, established, immovable], knowing that the same experiences of suffering are being experienced by your brothers and sisters throughout the world. [You do not suffer alone.] After you have suffered for a little while, the God of all grace [who imparts His blessing and favor], who called you to His own eternal glory in Christ, will Himself complete, confirm, strengthen, and establish you [making you what you ought to be]. To Him be dominion (power, authority, sovereignty) forever and ever. Amen.

Casting your care paints a colorful picture of taking what you have and throwing it into something else. In the Greek it's the exact same word used to describe the way Jesus' disciples threw their garments on the donkey He rode into Jerusalem. I want you to imagine your worry and anxiety as something tangible, like a garment you are wearing. Print out a silhouette of a shirt. Write all your cares and anxieties down and imagine taking off that garment of anxiety and throwing it onto Jesus. Place it on the cross symbolizing giving it to Him.

I want you to change your attitude regarding your healing in the area of mental health. You do not have to live with depression or anxiety. You can be free from being paranoid and bi-polar diseases. Don't stand for the things that come from the enemy. Don't make excuses for them. Don't leave any room for him to come in and take up residence. Cast out what you need to cast out. Talk about what needs to be talked about. Have the audacity to take a stand and decide NOT TODAY, SATAN!

Have the audacity to take a stand and decide NOT TODAY, SATAN!

Let's do some mental health work.

Diagnose yourself:

How am I feeling? Do I go to bed sad and wake up sad?

Is it internal? Is it external?

What are my thoughts?

What was my exposure recently? What have I watched, listened to or done.

Based on what you read, list any signs you have of depression.

Based on what you read list any signs you have of anxiety.

What has caused lasting stressors in your life?

What do you need to take off your plate before you add another thing?

Let's empty your emotional jug. (I recommend doing this with a friend, parent, pastor or mental health professional.)

CHAPTER FIVE

Labels Are for Boxes

It's not what they call you, it's what you answer to

-W.C. Fields

I get so fired up about the labels and stigmas people try to put on you. Classifications have been happening since elementary school. They classified us according to how we tested, acted, read and socialized. We were labeled smart, a good reader, a good student, a problem child, shy, hyperactive and whatever else they called us when we were not aware. Labels limit us and hinder possibilities. Be careful not to put yourself or other people in that imaginary box. Always remember, there is no box.

Labels limit us and hinder possibilities.

For instance, the term *single* mother is limiting. No, you are a mother. Don't take away from your motherhood just because a father is not present. That shouldn't hinder what you do as a mother. Yes, you are parenting alone, and I know that is not easy, but you don't need a father present to be a mother.

Don't let what people call you define you. You are not required to be what they call you and you don't have to line up within their lines of classification. I know I stay keeping people puzzled. I change regularly. I don't like that when it comes to politics the choices are so limited and you can't vote across parties. That is so unfair.

> Don't let what people call you define you.

Some days I agree with the democrats and some days I agree with the republicans. I never fully agree with either of them. I only fully agree with heaven. I do not like that I have to be identified as one or the other. When you choose independent there are times you can vote, so that forces you to choose a label. Outside of my race, gender and belief in God, I am never going to be one thing forever.

Have the audacity to evolve. It's ok to grow. You actually can become whoever you wish to become. You can become someone different based on your current revelation. Let's look at the scripture in Acts where Peter and John were labeled.

Acts 4:13 ESV

13 Now when they saw the boldness of Peter and John, and perceived that they were uneducated, common men, they were astonished. And they recognized that they had been with Jesus.

So, they were surprised at their boldness because they *perceived* they were uneducated and common. Man, if those aren't labels, I don't know what are. We experience transformation in Christ and like this scripture said they knew they had been with Jesus. But this transformation is ongoing. Who I am today, may not be who I am tomorrow. I will continue to change. The Bible says from one glory to another glory.

I think I really realized this while working on The National Reading Panel. I enjoyed this assignment and met some incredible educators, researchers, parents and children. The panel would evaluate existing research and evidence to find the best ways of teaching children to read. We traveled all around the country holding public hearings where people would give their opinions on what topics the panel should study. I enjoyed this work and appreciated the evolution of education that we were embarking on.

But what bothered me was the previous research I had to review. It was painful to see how they categorized children, education, gender, socioeconomic status, etc. I think I was most bothered when they decided previously which free books would go to what demographics and the type of books they sent. Just typing it disgusts me. They gave the areas that were "underserved" and "underprivileged" some of the worst material, in my opinion.

We would go into these neighborhoods and hear public comment from the community about the education being provided. I noticed something. These labels only existed in the minds of the people who created them.

I met some of the most intelligent, creative people in those areas they deemed "underserved." Lord, help me. I would tell them things like, go write your own books. Create your own narratives and stop looking for these people that you think are better than you to give you something. Tell your own stories. You are amazing and you have a voice.

Everyone, including me has their own way of learning and we don't all fit in the same box of how we should learn.

Times up for that old system of determining who we are and where we belong. We have to refuse the labels and start a new narrative that says who I am today is who I am supposed to be, and I will have the audacity to be who God called me to be.

Jesus always accepted those that society rejected. If He believed in labels, He would not have had dinner with tax collectors and lawyers or hung out with prostitutes and those caught in adultery. His actions certainly didn't line up with the notion that women are beneath men. He spoke to more women in His ministry than men. Jesus sees us all as one. No one is exalted above another because of who they are or where they came from.

Galatians 3:28

[28] *There is neither Jew nor Greek, there is neither bond nor free, there is neither male nor female: for ye are all one in Christ Jesus.*

Each day presents new possibilities. God never intended for us to stay the same. Beware of people who treat you like they met you. Saying things like, I remember when, or I can't believe you are such and such now. BELIEVE IT and I am not apologizing for where God has taken me.

I've been a pastor now for almost ten years. To date, I still have people from my pre-pastoring days giggle and say, "Girl, I can't believe you are a pastor." By now, you should know I am not hung up on titles, but there are people who purposely will not call me Pastor to keep me in their box. That is YOUR box not mine and it isn't hurting anyone but you. I am going to have the Audacity to be who God called me to be, unapologetically. Honestly, it's not how people see you that will hinder you, it's how you see yourself.

The number one thing that can hinder your destiny or keep you from being audacious is your past. The feeling that you don't deserve it, or you haven't done enough to obtain it. I wrote this great book called, *I'm Not That Woman*; you should get it.

The entire premise of the book is that your past has passed away. You can no longer access something that's no longer there, so why does your past keep coming up? Why do you feel unworthy? Why are shame and guilt in the emotional conversation? Because they come to kill destiny!

Don't ever apologize for how far God has brought you and don't hide or belittle it either. Some of us have the tendency to dim our lights in certain circles for fear of standing out and looking prideful. Let me tell you why that's dumb. Are you prideful? If your answer is no, then pride can't come from you. Also, the light you are shining is not yours, it's God's. You are His light. Stop making it about you and shine for Him. God will get the glory.

Matthew 5:14-16 TLB

14 You are the world's light—a city on a hill, glowing in the night
for all to see. 15-16 Don't hide your light! Let it shine for all; let
your good deeds glow for all to see, so that they will praise your
heavenly Father.

Don't hide your light for anyone. It's not your glory but God's glory. Men will praise God when they see you walking in who God created you to be. Don't downplay yourself because someone else is uncomfortable. You can't steal their shine because your light is different from theirs.

One of my favorite speeches to date was made by Angela Bassett, during the 2019 *Black Girls Rock* awards show. I feel like she transformed into the Queen Mother of Wakanda from the movie *Black Panther* when she delivered this amazing speech. Let's read an excerpt from this audacious speech:

"*So, when you're told you're not good enough, you tell them, not only am I good enough, I'm more than good enough,*" *she said.* "*When they say send her back home, you tell them I am home. I am the foundation of what you call home. When they tell you that you're angry or nasty, you tell them that they're mistaken. This is me. This is me being resolute and standing firmly in my truth. And when they say you're not beautiful, you tell them that you are the descendant of royalty.*"

I was screaming at my television, "SAY THAT, ANGELA!" I was so inspired by her speech. She ended with the famous passage from Romans chapter 8, "*If God be for us, who can be against us.*" My response to that is a resounding NOT ONE PERSON!

You are God's own handiwork, his workmanship. You were bought with a price, a high price. Trust that He who has begun a good work in you will complete it. He will fulfill His purpose for your life. He authored it and He will finish it. Believe that!

1 Peter 2:9 TLB

9 But you are not like that, for you have been chosen by God himself—you are priests of the King, you are holy and pure, you are God's very own—all this so that you may show to others how God called you out of the darkness into his wonderful light.

I am so passionate about people being who God made them to be, as I am sure you can tell by now. At a very young age I prayed and asked God to give me a daughter first. I wanted to have a daughter first because I thought it took more to raise a girl, due to my own emotional make-up. I knew Satan's strategies to make us feel insecure and less than, always trying to measure up to things that just aren't real.

I now know He doesn't just do that to women but men as well. He is just so jealous of mankind. In Psalm 8, he says, *What is man that you are so mindful of him.* With that thought, when I had my daughter, I would always tell her who she was even as an infant. I started early giving her quotes to build her self-image and singing songs to her about loving herself.

I remember we would watch American Idol together. Paris was like three years old. We loved watching it together. I heard a song written by Jessie J titled, Who You Are. Paris and I loved that song. The lyrics went something like this, "*I nearly left the real me on the shelf, no, no, no , no. Don't lose who you are, in the blur of the stars, seeing is deceiving, dreaming is believing, it's okay not to be okay, it's never too hard to follow your heart...Just be true to who you are.*"

I really liked the lyrics. I would sing them to her all the time, trying to get the message across to never try to be someone else, who you are is good enough. I think I played that song every night for months, looking in her eyes singing it to her. After the song ended, I would do my own little "Girl, let me tell you..." session, a format I adopted with young women while in youth ministry.

Those vulnerable sessions when you remove all the cosmetics and layers and just have real girl talk about real life issues plaguing us and providing real answers.

On a three-year-old level with my daughter it wasn't that deep, but I wanted her to understand that when you stare at your reflection you should always see beauty staring back. That was many years ago.

Fast forward to present day, she is now 12 and one night she was washing dishes as I was cleaning the counters. Like most people do when cleaning she was humming while washing. I listened a little closer to her hum; she was humming the tune of "Who You Are." I smiled and said, "Paris, do you know what you are humming?" She answered, "No, just something in my head." I smiled and said, "Mine too." Get a song in your head about yourself that will play throughout eternity and then sing it from your heart.

What is in your past that keeps trying to hijack your future?

Who do you dim your light around and why?

Write down some accomplishments that you've never celebrated.

Give God the glory and celebrate them.

CHAPTER SIX

Challenge Accepted

If it doesn't challenge you, it won't change you.

-Fred DeVito

I want you to make a promise. This promise will be to yourself and only you will know if you break it. I want you to accept a challenge you were afraid of or you have broken in the past. This challenge can be to stop eating sugar, (For some of you, I just cursed.) or apply for that new position. Or maybe it's simply breaking out of isolation and calling someone to hang out without the fear of rejection. Even if that is a fear, do it anyway.

Maybe you and your spouse are currently in a rough season; challenge yourself to tell them you love them every day or write them love notes. Whatever you decide I want you to do it for 30 days straight. If you miss a day, the next day is day one. I want you to develop better habits for yourself.

Yes, we will build in accountability soon because that is major, but this is for you to love yourself and practice being true and authentic to yourself with God as your main squeeze. By the way, one of the roles of the Holy Spirit is to be your helper. He can help. Lord knows, He has helped me. Don't do any of this without inviting Holy Spirit to help. Holy Spirit stands by waiting for you to ask for help.

John 14:26 AMP

26 But the [a]Helper (Comforter, Advocate, Intercessor—Counselor, Strengthener, Standby), the Holy Spirit, whom the Father will send in My name [in My place, to represent Me and act on My behalf], He will teach you all things. And He will help you remember everything that I have told you.

Never be afraid of a challenge. Challenge creates depth in your life. You see what you are made of. We don't know our full potential until we are stretched and pushed out of our comfort zone. You know the saying, If at first you don't succeed, try and try again. I believe that, I live that.

Never be afraid of a challenge. Challenge creates depth in your life.

Challenges are like traffic. They test your patience. If you let them really get to you, you will see no way out. But what I have learned is that good leaders play in traffic. People follow cars that find their way through congestion. We find alternate routes through our navigation systems (a type of Holy Spirit). I remember simply making use of the time. While I waited, I prayed, I worshipped, I listened to the Word. Just because you've been presented with an obstacle doesn't mean you can't overcome it.

Michael Jordan, considered by most as one of the greatest basketball players of all time, was cut from his high school basketball team because his coach didn't think he had enough skill.

Warren Buffet, one of the world's richest and most successful businessmen was rejected by Harvard University.

Steve Jobs was fired from the very company he started. His dismissal made him realize that his passion for his work exceeded the disappointment of what he thought was failure. He is even on record as saying getting fired from Apple was the best thing that could have ever happened to him.

Albert Einstein, literally known for intelligence—His name probably means genius—could not speak fluently until the age of nine. One of my favorite quotes from him is, "Failure is just success in progress."

Mickey Mouse creator Walt Disney was a high-school dropout who failed his attempt at joining the army. He was even fired from a Missouri newspaper for not being "creative enough." That literally makes me laugh.

The words "it had to happen" mean so much to me. We don't realize that some challenges in our lives were designed to reveal who we really are. A challenge is only a temporary setback that can set you up for a greater future. David said in Psalm 119:71 (TPT), "The punishment you brought me through was the best thing that could have happened to me, for it taught me your ways."

Challenges were designed to teach you something. You can give meaning to your challenges. What are you making them mean?

The meaning we attach to our stories either make us bitter or better. Does it mean you are not good enough, or does it mean you are not built to break? Stop asking, "Why me"? Why *not* you? If it would have never happened you wouldn't be who you are today. Look at you, you are not just a survivor but an overcomer.

Joseph can talk to us about challenges. He lived a life of challenges. His story starts with betrayal. His betrayal came from his own family. Betrayal, I won't lie, that's a big one. It is a silent killer because we suffer silently through disloyalty from a spouse, friend or family member.

If betrayal in our lives isn't processed correctly, our trust in others will erode over time producing doubt and low expectations of others. The shock that comes from deception and unfaithfulness can lead us into a vicious cycle and create mindsets within us that say betrayal is something we have to live with. Betrayal affects our subconscious minds making it difficult to live a limitless life.

Through Joseph's story we learn that you have to betray betrayal. I challenge you to jumpstart the healing process through forgiving. Forgiving doesn't mean you accept the wrong behavior; it means you release the person of the offense and detach from the pain, frustration and bitterness it produced.

Forgiveness is powerful. It breaks up from betrayal's bondage. Understand when trust is broken it is a process to regain. A chair may have broken on you when you sat in it. So, you don't quite trust that chair to sit in it again. It may need to be rebuilt, and that takes time. However, you can forgive that chair immediately for not handling you correctly.

Forgive them and work on building trust again. It's challenging, yes, but the new possibilities it makes space for in your life are priceless. Sometimes I think we don't forgive (especially when the betrayal was public) because of what people may think, people will say, or even because of your own declaration of, *If they ever do that, I will do that*. Then it's done. Grace shows up to forgive, but you don't receive it in fear that you will appear a certain way or betray your own resolve.

Joseph's story is beyond betrayal. Joseph's story starts out at a young age. He had a dream that he would be a leader of nations. Don't most of our stories start off like that, a dream, a word from God, a promise? Then here comes a challenge, uninvited like a thief in the night.

Joseph lived with four moms who shared one man. Imagine that. From those four moms twelve sons were produced of which he was the second youngest and his father's favorite. Being the favorite among twelve seems great until the others set out to kill you. His brothers hated him. They were jealous of him. Jealousy can make a person do irrational things. Their hate turned into malice and they decided one day to kill him.

While plotting his death an opportunity presented itself to sell him into slavery and ultimately, he was sold to Potiphar. Even while enslaved and betrayed by his own brothers, Joseph had the audacity to serve Potiphar with his whole entire heart as if he was meant to be there all along. Like somehow his betrayal set him on a course that God wanted him on.

Joseph again becoming acquainted with betrayal was wrongfully accused by Potiphar's wife of sexual assault. The system that was not built for him unjustly charged him and sent him to prison. Wow, I think of all those unjustly charged sitting in prison all across our country today because of a system not designed to protect them, but to incarcerate and institutionalize them. Joseph would say to those imprisoned like Afeni Shakur said to her son Tupac, "You may be in prison, but don't let the prison be in you. This prison cannot break you." Joseph demonstrated that by being promoted in jail to the right hand to the guy who ran the prison. Joseph met the cupbearer. He was Pharaoh's chief security. God gave him a dream and Joseph interpreted it. Isn't it wonderful to see that your gifts can still work in prison? Later Pharaoh was troubled by a dream and Joseph was remembered as an interpreter, which landed him a position that would set him up to be that leader of nations.

Understand that Joseph's story started with two dreams that followed up with numerous challenges. Joseph experienced 13 years of hurt and betrayal after his dream, but never grew bitter. How do we know that? He tells us.

I have always believed there is something in what you are named. Naming your children is important. Many of us name our children based on the story in which they were conceived or birthed, or even the journey it took to get them here. Names like Faith, Hope and Angel, typically have a story or a meaning behind them. In Genesis chapter 41:51 we see Joseph naming his sons. I believe the names he gave his sons speak to his journey.

His first son's name was Manasseh, it means one who causes to forget. Joseph was challenged to forget his betrayal and remember the promises of God. Your life will be determined by what you choose to remember and what you choose to forget.

In verse 52, we see him name his second son Ephraim. Ephraim means extra fruitful. It translates God has made me extra fruitful in the land of my affliction. Right there in the place that causes you the most pain, in the place of your betrayal, God will make you extra fruitful. Joseph would tell you not to curse the place where you are right now.

It may look challenging, *shoot*… it may *be* challenging. You may be in the pit, you may be wrongfully accused, you may even be in a prison, but God placed you in that place. Use the place that challenged you to strengthen you and place you where you dreamed you would be years ago. Don't run from the challenges, run through them.

Practically speaking, one of our greatest challenges is breaking bad habits. We establish many bad habits unconsciously and they come from triggers that we may have. For instance, emotional eating. Comfort food… that may be your go-to when your emotions are triggered. You give yourself permission because of how you are feeling. This is done very passively and unconsciously.

Here is the thing, your emotions don't have to be negatively triggered; you can eat because you are happy. You can eat because you feel like you should get a reward for being good all week. You feel accomplished that you ate fruit and veggies all week, so your feelings tell you that you *deserve those* two pieces of cake on Saturday and that ice cream on Sunday. Then your feelings really lie to you and say, you can always start over on Monday. Does that sound familiar? Ok, let's step away from food. Although it is so easy to use.

Think about Esau in Genesis chapter 25 who sold his entire

birthright for a piece of meat. Wasn't it food that caused the fall in Genesis chapter 3? Many followers of Jesus only followed him because he was always feeding them. Food is powerful and it can be a trap. That is why implementing fasting in your lifestyle is vital. It dethrones the "stomach god."

Putting food aside for real this time, let's talk about a challenge to develop a positive habit. A great habit we can all develop is our devotional life before God. How do I spend quality time with God in such a busy and distracting culture? Well in this instance, I would ask what is keeping you away from that time? Is it sleep? Not being able to get up early enough? Then you would need to make sure you go to bed earlier.

That means you need to re-evaluate your day and how you are spending your time. You may have to limit social media or take it out altogether for 30 days. Maybe cut back on television or talk radio time. Sometimes we cannot sleep because we need to declutter. Our minds are full of unnecessary thoughts that come from what we put in it during the day. Quite simply put, in order to spend more time with God, spend less time with the world. Simple but not easy.

> In order to spend more time with God, spend less time with the world. Simple but not easy.

The recipe for change in our lives is normally simple. Simple does not mean easy, nor does it mean fast. Most lasting changes that we have made actualized over time and it was difficult. Consistency outweighs intensity. We can all start off strong, but can we finish strong? It's why I said promise yourself something for 30 days. Go ahead and do it now.

One of our major pushbacks to change is other people. We want other people to change with us. When you start working out you think maybe my spouse should start too, and that is great, we are stronger together. But what if they don't? Will you still? What happens when people close to you don't support your change. Here is a resolve, you can't change anybody but you.

Stop looking for people to support your change or even be a part of your change. Yes, you can communicate your change to those you love, but watch your misguided expectations of them. Some things simply have to start with you, and you have to see it through. Trust me, your change will be inspiration and motivation for somebody tomorrow, but it may just be you and God today. Be ok with that.

Nobody sets out to live a mediocre life. Nobody strives to hear, *You are average.* God called us to live the abundant life, but it will not come without challenges. Don't back away from challenges. It is how we get better. Step up to the challenge. Don't stay the same all your life or wish you would have done something different.

What things can you do that you just really won't do because of fear? You may be really good at your job, but you have done it for over 20 years. I need you to realize that there is a whole world out there and people and things have evolved. Don't be afraid of evolution, even if it means you have to learn something new. You have the capacity to expand and stretch yourself. It makes room for more.

Isaiah 54:2 NLT

2 Enlarge your house; build an addition. Spread out your home, and spare no expense!

I love the way David stepped up to the challenge that was presented to him to defeat the Philistine in 1 Samuel chapter 17. When you think of this story, you think of David as the underdog. We think like that, but David didn't. He didn't see himself as "lesser" at all. As a matter of fact, neither David nor God called Goliath a giant. The Bible called him a champion of Gath, an uncircumcised Philistine. Sure, he was 9 feet 9 inches with a helmet of brass, armed with an exotic coat that weighed a ton. He had brass on his legs and between his shoulders was his spear, weighing 600 pounds, um… ok, that could all be a little intimidating. But David wasn't intimidated by what it looked like. He still stepped up to the challenge.

Here is the awesome thing. He didn't need anything outside of what he already had to defeat Goliath. We can be intimidated by what it looks like. We count ourselves out. We think the debt is too big, the job will require too much, the marriage is too hard, without ever stepping up to the challenge. And then we think we need something extra to overcome the challenge. David killed Goliath with a rock, a *rock*. What have you left alive that you need to kill? What is your rock?

There was a time I interviewed for a job that I had absolutely no qualification for. None😎, nada, zero, qualifications. A friend of the family told me about this position and said she knew the CEO pretty well. She told me she put in a good word for me and I was called in for an interview within a few days. I prayed about the position and I felt like the Lord said this was my job regardless of my experience or qualifications. Let me remind you, I did not have any experience and I wasn't qualified. When I arrived for the interview, I was a little intimidated, but I did not allow the feeling to stop me from stepping up to the challenge. I had a frog in my throat, and I told myself, that frog has to go before I open my mouth.

I sat in the chair across from my interviewer and answered the questions the best I could. I refused to say I didn't know anything. The Holy Spirit knows all things and He lives inside of me. I was just crazy bold back then. The more I talked and answered questions, the bolder and more confident I became. When the interview was over, I shook her hand and told her I would take the job and left. I was offered the job the next day. You do realize that was out of order.

It was years later when it was time to leave this job and move on to the next. My boss (the same lady that interviewed me) said to me, "I am sure going to miss you. I have never met anyone like you." She said when she first met me on that job interview that day, she thought to herself, *This girl is either really stupid or really smart.* I looked at her puzzled. "Why would you say that," I asked. She said, "You told me you would take the job before I offered it and even went as far as to ask me when you would start."

She told me I interviewed ok and she already had made up her mind on another candidate, but when I stepped up to the plate and told her I would take the job she changed her mind. Her words were, "This girl has the audacity to take a job that wasn't even offered to her."

If it doesn't challenge you, it won't change you.

Yes, that sounds like me, challenge accepted. God doesn't call the qualified, He qualifies the called. I am challenging you to step up and take the job before it's offered. Sometimes you need to be pushed into a challenge because if it doesn't challenge you, it won't change you.

I challenge you to love without measure.

I challenge you to live without limits.

I challenge you to breathe beyond betrayal.

I challenge you to work beyond failure.

I challenge you to run across borders.

I challenge you to defy all odds that are against you.

I challenge you to birth in spite of barrenness.

I challenge you to be still when you want to run.

I challenge you to reveal when you want to hide.

I challenge you to laugh at pain and turn it into promotion.

I challenge you to stay high when others are low.

I challenge you to pray without ceasing.

I challenge you to give without restraint.

I challenge you to break free while in prison.

I challenge you to dance like no one is watching.

I challenge you to dive into deep waters.

I challenge you to forgive like it never happened.

Accept the challenge. Let's do the work.

Write down three challenges that you are going to accept over the next 30 days.

Write down as many more as you can that Holy Spirit helps you come up with.

In what ways do you know God now that you didn't before the challenge?

What meaning have you given to some of your challenges?

For example, did you make your divorce mean you are not loved?

What have you left alive that you need to kill?

Write down the new habits you want to develop.

CHAPTER SEVEN

Die Empty

The wealthiest place on earth is the graveyard, because in the graveyard we will find inventions that we were never exposed to, ideas, dreams that never became a reality, hopes and aspirations that were never acted upon. -Myles Monroe

To date I have eulogized one person, my paternal grandmother, Ann Joppy. It was an honor to speak at her Homegoing service, but it was also a huge responsibility. I had the privilege of talking to her just days before she transitioned. Over the years we did not get to talk often, but when we did it was always very meaningful. Our last conversation she talked a lot about family, each of her children, her grandchildren, her great grandchildren and her great, great grandchildren. She talked about what was going on in their lives.

I was amazed about how much she knew. Even in her sickness she didn't miss a beat. But then she began to talk about me. I had never really talked to her about any ambitions or dreams that I had for my life. Every time we did talk, she was always expressing how proud she was of me and how she was hearing such great things about what I was doing. Especially in the community and in ministry.

Then she looked up at me with concern in her eyes. I had never seen this look on her before. She began to ask why I hadn't done things that were in my heart to do? (How in the world did she know?) She asked me what I was waiting for and had the nerve to have an attitude in her voice. She even went as far as to say, "There are so many people waiting for you. People in our own family."

As she spoke this, I was able to go beyond her words and hear clearly from heaven. This is what I heard, *Don't be satisfied with accomplishment. Once you complete one goal, set another one. I heard, Don't ever think you are finished. You are not finished until you die. I heard, There is more in there, do what you are scared to do.* (How in the world did she know about the fear?) It was like she was staring into my soul. As she was talking, I was moving. In my mind I was writing my first book, starting programs that I always wanted to start. I was repairing relationships. She was still talking, and I was already mobile. The last thing I heard, she didn't say it exactly like I heard it, but I heard-DIE EMPTY!

I shifted that day. That was the last time I would ever speak to my paternal grandmother. Three days later I got the call telling me she had transitioned, and she'd left instructions for me to eulogize her. I reflected on our conversation and knew what I had to do. I would continue the conversation she had with me. I would speak for her to our family. She empowered me and I was about to release a bomb. Listen in on the eulogy:

I won't be before you long (as most preachers say), my prayer is this next few minutes will provide a moment in your life that you will never get over. Many people say to you when someone transitions that you will mourn for a while but not always. While the mourning will pass, I pray that you never forget this time. Remember this day. NEVER GET OVER IT. Never get over how you feel right now. Why? Because whenever there is death it causes reflection. Death causes you to ask questions and even sometimes question God. We don't tend to have these conversations until someone we love is in a box in front of us.

You reflect on how you have lived up until now and where you will go from here. Somehow seeing someone you love pass on makes you think about your own eternal plans. Somehow you transition to your point of departure and ask yourself if you fulfilled your calling. Did you live beyond limitations? Did you affect anyone's life, or did you simply live for yourself? Grandma sure didn't. She literally lived for us. I even believe in her last days she held on just so some of us could see her for the last time and have closure.

In my last moments with her she encouraged me to die empty. At least that was my takeaway. It reminded me of a passage that I often meditate on:

Joshua 11:15 MSG

Just as God commanded his servant Moses, so Moses commanded Joshua, and Joshua did it. ***He didn't leave incomplete one thing that God had commanded Moses. [emphasis added]***

In my heart that scripture now literally reads, Just as God commanded his servant ANN, so ANN commanded Portia and Portia did it. She didn't leave incomplete one thing that God commanded her.

If Grandma was here today, she would tell you, "Leave nothing incomplete. Finish everything that God has put in your heart and eliminate every excuse. Stop coming short of the finish line because of obstacles. You are an overcomer. The life you are living right now you were built for. Go back and slay every enemy that thought they took you out. Come out of hiding and show them who you are."

Hear her saying, "Take up my mantle, it's the only thing I am leaving in the Earth. See there is an awesome story in the Bible that can be found in 2 Kings chapter 2 verse 14 about a prophet that transitioned to heaven and just like many of us, God allowed his servant to be there as he transitioned. As he was ascending to heaven he told Elijah, "If you can see it, you can have it." Which means when I leave, there is a mantle that will be left. But you have to be able to "see" it."

What did you see in Grandma's life that you can have? Many of us don't walk in it and don't receive it because we are blinded. We allow for the generational curses, instead of the blessings because that is all we see. But the curse only lingers because no one will take responsibility for it. When I say take responsibility, I am saying be RESPONSE ABLE.

You are able to properly respond when the curse tries to show up to defeat you. It may not be your fault, but you can take responsibility and END IT. The curse of poverty, the curse of bad relationships, infidelity and divorce. The curse of addiction and mental health disorders. I want you for a moment to think about the first family, Adam and Eve. The curse was only allowed to exist in the Earth because they would not take responsibility for their actions. They played the blame game. Listen to this:

Genesis 3:11-13

[11] *And he said, Who told thee that thou wast naked? Hast thou eaten of the tree, whereof I commanded thee that thou shouldest not eat?*

[12] ***And the man said, The woman [Emphasis added]****whom thou gavest to be with me, she gave me of the tree, and I did eat.*

[13] *And the LORD God said unto the woman, What is this that thou hast done?* ***And the woman said, The serpent*** *beguiled me, and I did eat.* ***[Emphasis added]***

Adam blamed Eve and Eve blamed the devil, as a result a curse was released. We cannot go through life blaming anyone. When you take responsibility you say, "Listen, this stops here." Apply the blood of Jesus to every curse lived out in your family and receive wholeness in those areas. You will now see the blessings. When Jesus died, He became sin to dissolve the curse and leave the blessing. So, we get all of the blessings and none of the curses. Grandma would say the same thing.

"The curse of not finishing dies with me. Look at the blessing on my life. I am leaving that." Every parent desires to pass down all of the good and none of the bad. The greatest good grandma did was receive Jesus Christ as her Lord and Savior. You cannot give anything away to your children that you don't have. You want them to live a better life than you, well you have to live a better life. Grandma knew she would only live better if she made Jesus Lord. She did that, can you see it? Can you see the blessings as a result of it? She lived out her purpose in the Earth. But she would tell you she didn't start living until she received Him. Her greatest desire is that you receive Him.

Isaiah 57:1-2 NLT

Good people pass away; the godly often die before their time. But no one seems to care or wonder why. No one seems to understand that God is protecting them from the evil to come. For those who follow godly paths will rest in peace when they die.

I want you to notice that in this passage of scripture there is a distinction between the good and the Godly. Both will die but "those who follow Godly paths will Rest in Peace when they die." Grandma can Rest In Peace because she followed a Godly path. Godly people die in purpose. What will her death symbolize in your life? She died empty. Peace means nothing lacking or missing. It is finished, complete. It is appointed for every man to die. Can you say you will Rest In Peace?

Over 40 people gave their lives to the Lord that day. I cannot tell you the overwhelming since of joy I felt. I knew God was happy and Grandma was smiling while finally resting.

We cannot talk about courage without talking about my boy Joshua, my prototype. We read about Joshua primarily in the Book of Joshua. I know when I read about his life, I am fascinated by his stance. His ability to move, to get the job done without fear. Moses was a good leader, but he was a bit of a people pleaser. He allowed people and their complaining to keep him from seeing the Promised Land. When Joshua stepped up as leader, God said something to him that always has given me chills.

Joshua 1:2

2 Moses my servant is dead; now therefore arise, go over this

Jordan, thou, and all this people, unto the land which I do give to them, even to the children of Israel.

When something or someone dies, new life is always waiting. God was saying Moses' time has come to an end. It's your time! It's time for new beginnings. Now Moses was an amazing leader. To lead people through the wilderness is no easy feat. He was the first who saw God's face, experienced His presence. He experienced the most amazing miracles during his time. Under his leadership the Red Sea was parted, one of the greatest miracles on record.

But now it was time to cross over. To go into the Promised Land and God chose Joshua.

I thought Joshua was a great person to talk about to close my book on Audacity. He is one of the most audacious people we read about in the word of God.

Portia: *Joshua, it seems like Moses' death was unexpected. How did you prepare to replace him? Were you afraid?*

Joshua: *I could never replace Moses. It was simply my time. I know this sounds cliché, but I was born ready. I had to stay ready. But I have to be honest, there was a reason why you read "be courageous" four times. God knew what was really going on within me.*

Being Moses' assistant I learned a lot, I saw a lot. I was appreciative for who he was in my life and I honored him. Portia, tell people to honor the old when they take the baton into the new. We would not be who we are without those who laid the path for us. Honor is important.

People don't realize I was a slave in Egypt too. I grew up a slave. I wasn't born in Canaan, I was born into slavery, beaten by taskmasters. I was a slave, but I was never enslaved. Instead of complaining, learn to take lessons learned from every season and situation you find yourself in and then use them. Even when you feel beat down find the strength to keep moving forward.

I am an observer, I learned from good and bad leadership. It may sound harsh, but it was in slavery where I learned you can shift mindsets. See, you view me as confrontational. I am, but I never focused on the people's shortcomings in order to cross over into the Promised Land. No, I had to create a world where there was none. You become what you focus on. You can't move forward looking back. Don't live life looking in the rearview mirror, because eventually you will crash.

I had to have a growth mindset that said the bigger the challenge, the more we have the capacity to stretch. I learned how to see different. You remember when Moses sent us to Canaan? Ten spies had the wrong mindset. Mindsets change the meaning of things. The land to them was occupied by giants and we were grasshoppers in their sight, according to them. I didn't get that memo. That is still funny to me today.

I saw something completely different. Caleb and I were excited, we figured the men were that big because of all the milk and honey they had in Canaan. Portia, the grapes were so big, and we were hungry, our mindset was—we all about to eat! We are well able to possess this land! When you hungry you see different. Tell the people in your generation, they not hungry enough.

Portia: *Boy, you crazy! Talk to me about how you covered more ground in less time.*

Joshua: *I learned that some things will not be successful because of principles but because of presence. It is how we defeated Jericho. By the shout, praising God and evoking His presence. Have the audacity to look crazy in seemingly impossible situations. I will always remember what the Lord said to me in the beginning. "As I was with Moses, I will be with you." Portia, I could not do anything without Him. I knew as long as He was with me, I could do anything.*

What was most important to me as a leader was the courage to follow God and not the people. So yes, where you saw me throughout my time making bold declarations and giving the people ultimatums, it was because I had to keep the enemy out of my camp. We only serve one God and I refused to bow to any other. You have to give all your fears, insecurities and anybody that likes to entertain the enemy, your declarations and ultimatums. You cannot allow that stuff to hang out in your camp. Draw a line in the sand, like I did. Tell everyone and everything, If you are with me then step on this side with me, but if you want to serve other things, stay on the other side and watch the Earth swallow you up.

I believe I covered more land in a shorter time because I had the audacity to follow God. I was born Hoshea, but Moses, following God's instruction changed my name to Joshua—a follower of God. My name literally means salvation. Portia, sometimes you have to change your name to walk in who you really are. Abraham, Sarah, Jacob all had name changes.

How did I enter the Promised Land? I had the audacity to be who God called me to be.

Portia: Thanks, Joshua. Can you close my book with some benediction-like nuggets😊?

Joshua: To your readers, you are equipped with everything you need to possess what God has for you. Don't allow paralysis to keep you stuck. There is new territory for you to take. I can see you. I see your strength, your love, your passion and your audacity. Nothing is insignificant where you are concerned. Keep the mind of Christ as you journey, accept every challenge and leave nothing incomplete. Die empty!

Numbers 6:22-26 NIV

The LORD said to Moses, "Tell Aaron and his sons, 'This is how you are to bless the Israelites. Say to them: *"The LORD bless you and keep you; the LORD make his face shine on you and be gracious to you; the LORD turn his face toward you and give you peace."*

End Notes:

Chris Hodges, Fresh Air

Rick Warren, Purpose Driven Life

Carolyn Dwek, Ph.D., Mindset

Dennis and Dr. Jen Clark, Self Deliverance Made Easy

Stephen S. Ilardi, Ph.D., The Depression Cure

Myles Monroe, In Pursuit of Purpose

CPSIA information can be obtained
at www.ICGtesting.com
Printed in the USA
FFHW011154240120
58027822-63158FF